PRAISE FOR LAWRENCE GROBEL

THE H "A Masterpiece." —James A. Michener. "Extensive ar *York Times.* "The best book of the year."- mantic, exciting and compellin

CO rfully outrageous rea –*The Denver Post*

CC e!"—Marlon Brando

AL PACINO ***Grobel:*** "Journalist Grobel, who literally wro viewing, puts his talents on full display...giving the rea uch insight into interviewing style as into the legendary actor... Part of the book's draw is witnessing the two become closer as the years go by...making for increasingly engaging and illuminating reading."—*Publisher's Weekly* Starred Review

THE ART OF THE INTERVIEW: Lessons from a Master of the Craft: "Grobel gives readers the equivalent of a master class in this thoroughly entertaining treatise on one of the toughest tasks in journalism.... *The Art of the Interview* is an overstuffed treat, full of anecdotes, advice from other top writers and the kind of commiserating stories about difficult editors, hellish assignments and prickly stars that will seize the attention of both professional interviewers and their audiences."—*Publisher's Weekly*

ABOVE THE LINE: CONVERSATIONS ABOUT THE MOVIES: "This book satisfies on every level. I ate my copy and feel very full."—Steve Martin. "A diverse and lively collection, the highest art of the interview."—Joyce Carol Oates. "There are passages in this book that will leave you stunned." —Dylan McDermott. "In his quiet, conversational way, Larry gets people to talk about things they'd rather not talk about."—Elmore Leonard

ENDANGERED SPECIES: Writers Talk About Their Craft, Their Visions, Their Lives: "As an interviewer Larry's all the things Joyce Carol Oates has said he is: prepared, adaptable, and graced with the intelligence needed to shoot the breeze and elicit intriguing responses from uncommonly gifted and often uncommonly suspicious subjects."—Robert Towne

CLIMBING HIGHER (for Montel Williams): "An absolutely riveting read."—*N. Y. Post*

CATCH A FALLEN STAR: "...keeps the reader in suspense from the first cannon shot to the finale in this perceptive understanding of the illusion and the reality of the movie capital of the world." —*DZIENNIK,* 5 Star Review

YOU SHOW ME YOURS: "Profoundly entertaining."—Diane Keaton

Also by Lawrence Grobel

Fiction
Catch a Fallen Star
Begin Again Finnegan
The Black Eyes of Akbah
Commando Ex

Memoir
You Show Me Yours

Nonfiction
Signing In: 50 Celebrity Profiles
"I Want You in My Movie!" The Making of Al Pacino's Wilde Salome
Yoga? No! Shmoga!
Icons: 15 Celebrity Profiles
Marilyn & Me (for Lawrence Schiller)
Al Pacino: In Conversation with Lawrence Grobel
Conversations with Robert Evans
The Art of the Interview: Lessons from a Master of the Craft
Climbing Higher (with Montel Williams)
Endangered Species: Writers Talk About Their Craft, Their Vision, Their Lives
Above the Line: Conversations About the Movies
Conversations with Michener
The Hustons
Conversations with Brando
Conversations with Capote

Poetry
Madonna Paints a Mustache & Other Poems

Conversations
with Ava Gardner

■ ■ ■

Lawrence Grobel

First Edition

Text copyright © 2014 Lawrence Grobel
www.lawrencegrobel.com

All rights reserved.
No part of this book may be reproduced in any form or by any electronic or mechanical means, including information storage and retrieval systems without written permission from the author except by a reviewer who may quote passages in a review.

Cover design: Paul Singer.

Ava Gardner photos: Used with permission, The Ava Gardner Trust

ISBN-13: 9781500635428

To all the free-spirited women in my life—
Hiromi, Maya, Hana, Roberta, Mayumi, Mari,
Marlene, Lori, Rita, Marta, Ajoa, Christie, Diane
& Joyce

"Life is trouble; only death is not. To be alive is
to undo your belt and look for trouble!"
–Nikos Kazantzakis, *Zorba the Greek*

Contents

1	A Rootless, Beautiful Stray	1
2	"Before I Die"	43
3	The Ground Under Her Toes	61
4	Just a Pretty Little Girl in Hollywood	94
5	The Billionaire & the Clarinet Player	113
6	Ol' Blue Eyes & the Gift Giver	125
7	A Real-Life Contessa, Hurtfully Wounded	145
	Bio	163
	Excerpt from *Conversations with Brando*	164
	Other Books	187

1

A Rootless, Beautiful Stray

IT WAS JOHN HUSTON WHO BROUGHT ME TO AVA. He was an old man then, inhaling oxygen through a tube connected to a portable tank, but when her name came up his eyes brightened, even moistened, and he remembered her well. Anyone who ever met her remembered her well. She was unlike any other movie star of her era. There may have been a few who were as beautiful, but none more beautiful. And none as full of life or as carefree. She was a woman men desired and women admired.

I was writing a book about Huston's family, and he had written a letter on my behalf, indicating his full support of my endeavor to interview everyone in his three address books. If they knew him, worked with him, fought with him, wrote for him, loved him or hated him, I wanted to talk to them. Ava Gardner's London address was in his book.

"I was interested in her," Huston admitted to me when we spoke about *The Killers*, which he wrote in 1946 with Anthony Veiller. "May have even married her, who knows? But the night I made a move, she ran away. The Bucks had brought her out to my house in the Valley a few days after we had previewed *The Killers*, which she was in with Burt Lancaster and Edmund O'Brien. Jules Buck was one of the producers. We had a grand evening. Ava was radiant. I could hardly take my eyes off her. After a few drinks, she and I went outside to the backyard. I couldn't contain myself; I'm not ashamed to admit that. She was standing under the glow of the moonlight like a Greek statue, her skin seemed to shimmer, and she was like an enchantress. And I was entranced. When I went towards her she began to run, which I took as her being playful, so I ran after her. She ran between the trees, and then she circled the swimming pool, with me in pursuit. But she was elusive and though she was laughing, I sensed that she wasn't going to allow me to capture her. When I got close she dove into the pool, fully clothed. I stood there and laughed with her. The next day I went off to Las Vegas and married Evelyn Keyes. But I doubt that would have happened had Ava not jumped in that pool."

I asked Ava about that story when we first met at her home at 34 Ennismore Gardens in London on July 15, 1986. "Oh John," she laughed. "I love John Huston. Such a rascal. Yes, that happened, he chased me. We both had too much to drink. He chased me around the bushes behind his house. It was a big joke. I remember diving into the pool. I knew if I didn't dive in I would have been in trouble. John was a great womanizer and I wasn't the kind of gal who liked to be womanized. I knew he wasn't serious; he was just looking for a good time. He asked me to spend the night but it was already almost dawn when we left with John standing in the doorway waving goodbye. And Jules and Joyce Buck were saying, 'Oh, poor John.' But yes, it's true, later that day he went off to Las Vegas with Evelyn."

Ava was 24 at that time and had already divorced Mickey Rooney, turned down Howard Hughes's proposals, and was unhappily married to Artie Shaw, but we would talk about those men in due time.

I noticed that my hand was shaking when I first went to ring her doorbell. She had a reputation for not liking journalists and for very rarely sitting for an interview. But when Huston had written, "Larry has my full support to contact those of my friends and associates whom he feels will be useful to his task. I trust they will offer a true memory and fresh perspective to the telling of my past years," she took it as another of his directions. And, being an obedient actress (at least for this particular director), she was following directions. "Come on in!" she called and I opened the door. She was standing at the top of the stairs, wearing a white blouse and floral pattern pink skirt, with her dog Morgan, a corgi, barking by her feet. "He'll just sniff you," she said. "A lot of bark, no bite."

She was forty years older than when John Huston had chased her around the swimming pool but she was still Ava Gardner, made up and looking good with that fine skin and dimpled chin. "Let's have a drink," she said as we sat by the fireplace in her living room. She opened a bottle of white wine and brought two glasses with ice in them which she swished around, then poured the wine. "These are pretty good," she said, submerging a hard boiled quail egg in a dip she had prepared and then popping it in her mouth. "Go on, try one. Get comfortable before we talk about my friend John."

I bent down and brought a tape recorder from my bag and her demeanor changed completely. She looked at it with distaste and slight horror when I put it on the coffee table between us. I thought she might choke on the quail egg.

"I can't talk into those things," she said. "If I see it, I freeze up. I go ABSOLUTELY to pieces! I'm petrified. Turn it off."

"No," I protested, "Don't even think about it." I had run into this problem with other stars, among them Mae West, Al Pacino, George C. Scott and Jerry Lewis, as well as with producer Ray Stark, but had managed to convince all but Mae West to allow me to record our conversations. My method was to make light of it. But Ava wasn't treating it lightly.

"That's one of the main reasons, one of the drawbacks, why I haven't done a book. Because I can't talk into one of those. I'm useless at doing these things. The closer I am to one of those machines the worse it is. You must turn it off."

I put the recorder under the table, out of her sight. It was still on, which she knew, but she didn't protest. We spent the rest of the afternoon talking as if it wasn't there.

"You know," she said, "that John didn't get a writing credit for *The Killers*. I didn't know that he had written it with Tony Veiller until that night at his house, after we had screened it. I think it had something to do with his being in the army or being under contract to Warner Bros."

"That picture kind of did it for you," I said. In the story, based on Ernest Hemingway's short story, two hired thugs come to a diner waiting for "the Swede" to appear so they can kill him. Hemingway didn't give any back story, but in the film we learn that the Swede was a former boxer who had fallen for this beautiful woman and committed a robbery for her, then double-crossed those he worked for and got double-crossed by the woman. He has nothing left to live for. Ava played the beautiful double-crossing woman. "You were featured in all the publicity; you were shown on all the billboards and posters. And your femme fatale character was established."

"Oh what the hell did I know?" she said. "I went to the set the first day in full makeup and the director told me to take it off. So I did the film without makeup. That was a relief."

"How many actresses could say that?" I smiled.

"I had nothing to do with it, honey. I was born that way. I had nothing to do with anything I did. I never understood why I was so famous."

"I know you say that," I said. "But I wonder if you really mean it. Because you have been really famous since *The Killers*, and that was back in 1946."

"Fame ain't what it's cracked up to be, let me tell you. It's a pain in the ass if you ask me. You've been talking to all these people who worked with John, a lot of them famous. How many are happy, well-adjusted, or even satisfied with their lives? Very few, I can tell you that."

"Yes, but how many would give up their fame for anonymity? Very few, I bet."

"I'd be one of them," she laughed. "Believe me. In a fucking minute."

Other than mentioning that *The Killers* was "an excellent film" and that it was Burt Lancaster's first movie, Ava didn't much care to talk about it. I think she just felt that they hired her because of her looks and that she still felt, all these years later, that she wasn't much of an actress. She knew how to look sultry and desirable, she had certainly been taught to pose that way by so many accomplished photographers, and she probably would have agreed with Pauline Kael's assessment of her that was written in 1974, when Kael was reviewing *Earthquake*:

"Gardner was one of the last of the woman stars to make it on beauty alone. She never looked really happy in her movies; she wasn't quite there, but she never suggested that she was anywhere else, either. She had a dreamy, hurt quality, a generously modeled mouth, and faraway eyes. Maybe what turned people on was that her sensuality was developed but her personality wasn't. She was a rootless, beautiful stray, somehow incomplete but never ordinary, and just about impossible to dislike, since she was utterly without affectation."

So instead of trying to pry her with technical movie questions, I went off topic and asked her about Hemingway, since besides *The Killers*, she had made two other films based on his stories: *The Snows of Kilimanjaro* in 1952 and *The Sun Also Rises* in 1957.

"I adored Ernest Hemingway," she said. "I met him when I was in the hospital with kidney stones in Madrid in 1954, after Frank (Sinatra), when I was with Luis Miguel. That was a thrill."

"Sounds painful," I said.

"Ha! I was in hell for a week. It was more of a clinic than a hospital. And there were nuns who kept putting blankets on the floor, because you can't sit still when you have kidney stones, and I had two of them, one in each kidney. Excruciating agony. Thank God for Luis Miguel."

She was talking about Dominguin, the most famous bullfighter in Spain at the time, who was also her lover. They had gone out for dinner and when they got home, "This horrible pain started. He knew right away what it was because his brother had had it. It was like the worst menstrual pains only low in the stomach. A very sharp, dulling pain. They put me in a warm bath and I thrashed around in that. Miguel knew some kidney specialist who came, but he damn near ruined my kidneys because they kept filling me with water which just swelled me up. The water was backing up in my kidneys, which could have poisoned me. And all these doctors and their old friends would come to my room to visit, puffing their cigars, drinking, looking at me and saying 'Oh, isn't she beautiful.' It was like a fucking nightclub!

"My sister Bappie was there. They put a cot in my room for Luis Miguel, who stayed with me those two weeks instead of going to the bullfight festival in San Isidro. But my condition kept getting worse. I was so swollen with all the liquids. They decided to do an x-ray, and put a catheter inside me, but I couldn't sit still for it, so they tried to hold me down. But if anybody tries to restrain me I go crazy. I go absolutely insane! That goes back to my father, but that's another story. They were trying to hold me, and I was screaming with all the pain and the terror. Finally Miguel came in and started shouting that they should leave me alone and take their hands off me. He sat next to me, took my hand, and kept very, very quiet. He sat with me when they took the x-ray, and he came into the operating room where they gave me an injection. I think it was sodium pentothal, because they left the needle in my arm in case I needed more. When they went in with the catheter they hit one of the stones and just pushed it back, so that made the pain even worse. I tore the needle from my arm. It was really a fuck-up and I was lucky that I didn't get a terrible kidney infection."

"This is some way to meet Hemingway," I said. "I read that you actually gave him one of the stones."

"I don't believe that. The stories that people write are absolutely mind-boggling. Here's what happened. One afternoon Miguel and Bappie went to the bullfights. Miguel wasn't fighting any more; he was retired. Hemingway and Miss Mary were there, and when Miguel came to my room he said, 'I have a surprise for you.' And there was Papa. He was my idol. And all of a sudden, my pain disappeared. He was a wonderful old man, just what you wanted him to be with his gray beard. But he didn't look very well because he had been through an accident in Africa. It was his first trip back to Spain since Franco, because he wasn't allowed back since he had fought on the wrong side during the Civil War. He was thrilled to be back. And I was thrilled to see him. He stayed for a couple of hours, sitting on a chair, drinking, chatting. He called me 'Daughter' right from the start, which reminded me of my father, who always called me Daughter. He told me about the African trip the month before, when his plane went down and he and Miss Mary were almost killed. But he didn't make a big drama out of it. Not as much as the drama I made with my kidney stones."

"So Hemingway didn't ask you for a souvenir stone?"

"No, they hadn't flushed until days later and we didn't catch either of them, they just suddenly came. It's important to catch the stone to find out what it consists of. But I've had to be very careful of calcium since then. Even though, when I was in Los Angeles, I was being treated by this doctor who thought it a good idea to give calcium shots intravenously. That's a most peculiar feeling. It's a terrible burning sensation as it goes into the vein, which starts strangely enough in the vagina, and your whole body is flushed. Horrible feeling. But that was one of those periods when doctors were trying all sorts of things and I'm a trusting fool."

We had gone from her kidney stones to Dominguin to a glimpse of Hemingway and over to Los Angeles for calcium shots that burned her vagina. Ava had a stream-of-conscious way of talking. You just had to settle in and roll along.

"If you believe the press, Papa and I were bosom buddies over the years," she said, returning to Hemingway. "But that wasn't true at all. I just saw him and Miss Mary periodically, when they came to Spain, and I visited them in New York and Cuba. But just knowing him a little bit made a tremendous impact. I saw Miss Mary more than I did him. They had a wonderful relationship. He would have those fits, which she absolutely ignored; it didn't bother her in the least. She was a brilliant woman and could have been a damn good writer too. It was definitely Papa's most successful marriage. I hear the others were disasters, like mine."

"So there was no sexual attraction between you and Hemingway?" I had to ask.

"As I say, I didn't know him that well. But he had that sort of animal quality that would appeal to me. I'm sure he was sexually attractive when he was young because I'd seen photographs of him and he was so handsome. I also happen to know that he was really hung."

I wondered how she knew that, if she didn't know him "that well."

"Reenie and I went down to Havana to go fishing with Papa." Reenie was Mearene Jordan, who went to work for Ava in 1947 and became her close friend and confidante. "We went to his house and took a boat out and went fishing. Now I ain't much of a fisherman, honey, so we all sat and drank rum. Reenie got seasick and went below to lie down. Papa didn't know she was there and went to change his clothes. When we got back to shore, Reenie couldn't wait to tell me, 'Lord's a mercy, Miss G, no wonder all these women went crazy—that man is really hung!' So Reenie was very impressed with Papa's genitals."

"Did you ever tease Papa about it?"

"You didn't tease Papa—that man had a temper. But drunk or sober he was something special. Afterwards we went into a very famous place that is practically named for him, filled with his photographs. Wonderful food. We got very drunk that night. I remember he told me how much he didn't care about movies, though he said he liked *The Killers* and the one about the Spanish Civil War, *For Whom the Bell Tolls*. And he approved of *The Old Man and the Sea*. But most of them he absolutely hated—just hated what they did to his stories."

I brought up *The Sun Also Rises*, which I had read as a teenager and really liked. "I love his writing," Ava said. She played Lady Brett Ashley in the movie, a freewheeling woman who falls in love with Jake Barnes, the one man who can't physically return her love because he is impotent. ("Brett was damned good-looking," Hemingway wrote. "She was built with curves like the hull of a racing yacht.") "The movie was sort of a mess. When they sent me the script I didn't think it did the book justice and I wanted to take it to show him, hoping he might fix it. But I was told not to take it to him. I did anyway, and boy, he was furious. He was living up in Escorial, near the old palace and museums. He was really in his cups and got terribly rude. Oh, he could be rude! He was awful, used foul language, and he picked on the people he loved the most. Miss Mary—oh my God. Peter Viertel had written a version of the script and Papa adored Peter. But he didn't adore the script I brought him to read. Papa was in bed, talking to me, when Miss Mary walked in. We had been drinking and Papa ignored Miss Mary. She said, 'Papa, aren't you going to salute me?' With that, he stood up in the bed in his old pajamas and said, 'I salute you, bitch.' And then he started making a couple of speeches, talking about the trip to Africa when his plane went down. I left him alone to read the script and when he had, the thing that upset him more than anything, he said, was the failure of authenticity. Regarding the plane, he said, 'The stupid fools; they are using a kind of aircraft that wasn't even invented in those days.' The technicalities upset him the most."

I thought that mentioning the time John Huston visited Hemingway in Cuba in 1948 would be a good transition to getting back to Ava working with Huston in Puerto Vallarta and Mismaloya, Mexico for *The Night of the Iguana*. That was especially so since the Huston/Hemingway episode involved shooting an iguana. Huston was a huge admirer of Hemingway. "The best that I can get out of a scene," Huston had said, "is when it stops being something that you're looking at and becomes an experience. In literature this happens rarely, but when it does it's extraordinary. Certain American writers have a penchant for this, a peculiar ability to re-create, to make you feel that you're actually present in something. If Hemingway had anything, he had that."

It was Peter Viertel who had brought Huston down to meet Hemingway and they all went fishing. An iguana was spotted on a rock, and either Huston or Hemingway took a shot and wounded the animal. Huston told me it was Hemingway who took the shot, but Evelyn Keyes, who was also there, said it was John. Either way, Hemingway insisted that the iguana be tracked and properly killed. Huston and Viertel went to do it, but after two hours they gave up. Hemingway wasn't satisfied and went himself in the broiling sun and managed to find the iguana and put him out of his misery. Huston was impressed with Papa's persistence and determination.

"I guess you can call that the Last Day of the Iguana," Ava laughed. "How's your drink, Hon? You're not much of a drinker, are you?"

"I'm still working," I reminded Ava. "How'd John get you to do *The Night of the Iguana*?"

"John called me, said he and his producer Ray Stark were in Madrid. I hadn't talked to John since he chased me around his swimming pool all those years ago and I had just made three pictures that I wasn't very fond of (*The Angel Wore Red, 55 Days at Peking,* and *Seven Days in May*), so I really wasn't interested in making another one when he called. But John has a way of seducing you with his charming voice. He wanted me to show them a good time, and I was always up for that."

The good time lasted three days and nights, as Ava took them to different nightclubs where they drank and watched flamenco dancers and Ava danced as Huston and Stark clapped as fast as they could. Any talk of casting her in *Iguana* was put aside as the men surrendered themselves to Ava's world.

The part they wanted her to play was Mrs. Maxine Faulk, the proprietor of a rundown tourist hotel on the coast of Mexico. As Tennessee Williams described her, she was "a stout, swarthy woman in her middle forties—affable and rapaciously lusty. She is wearing a pair of levis and a blouse that is half unbuttoned."

Bette Davis had played her on stage. Williams' story was about human frailty and how we manage to survive all the pitfalls that life throws our way. It centers around a quirky cast of characters. There's the renegade, fallen clergyman named T. Lawrence Shannon, whose penchant for liquor and young girls finds him desperately trying to cling to his final job–leading a tourist bus of Texas schoolteachers from a Baptist Female College around the Mexican coast. There's a New England spinster, Hannah Jelkes, who travels with her 97-year-old grandfather Nonno, "the world's oldest living and practicing poet." There's a beautiful teenage girl, under the guardianship of the schoolteachers, who is there to tempt Shannon to fall even lower. And there's the iguana, chained to a post, symbolizing the bondage all of these characters are caught in. Huston and Stark had already flown to Switzerland to convince Richard Burton to play the defrocked reverend—"a man," Huston said, "desperate and full of despair, at the end of his rope." Then they went to London to cast Deborah Kerr as the New England spinster. Ava was next on their list.

"I knew damn well that Ava was going to do it," Huston had told me. "She did too—but she wanted to be courted. So we went out with my beloved Ava three nights running. She lived a very rigorous existence, I must say. We'd meet in the afternoon, have drinks, then go to dinner around ten o'clock. After dining, it was the clubs and the dancing, and this would go on all night. Ray was made of stronger stuff than I—not quite of the mettle and fiber of Ava, who was quite capable of going on through that night and through the next day and the next night and the next! I presently dropped out and Ray went on as her escort for several nights until we left Madrid."

"What nights those were!" Ava laughed. "I took them to flamenco joints and we stayed up all night long, drinking rotten brandy and anise, not talking about the picture at all. In fact, I almost talked Huston out of it. I'm sure if Ray Stark had appeared on his own it would have pushed me the other way, to run. Ray was a typical agent/hustler type. His approach was not the approach that would have swayed me. I would have said, 'Okay, let's go out and get drunk and see a flamenco,' and that would have been the end of it. I really didn't want to work. I was going through a phase in my life. I was trying to get away from the whole thing. But with Huston it was hard to say no. He didn't sit and say, 'You must do this, this is good for you'—none of that crap. He never mentioned anything. Which was the same way he directed."

Stark smiled fondly when asked about courting Ava in Madrid. "She wore us out," he said. "I never thought I'd see the day when someone could out-drink and outlast John Huston, but Ava was in a class by herself. Even when she agreed to do the picture, I was in contact with Melina Mercouri as a backup, in case Ava sobered up and didn't remember saying yes."

When Ava did sober up she realized that she was about to fly into a circus-like atmosphere, with Elizabeth Taylor accompanying Burton, Viertel with his wife Deborah Kerr, 19 year-old Sue Lyon coming off her starring role in *Lolita*, Huston and what he brought to the table, and Tennessee Williams, who disagreed with the ending Huston had decided on but went down to protect as much of the story as he could. Huston knew the press would have a field day with this crew and decided to make the film in as remote a place as possible, which is why he chose Puerto Vallarta and not Acapulco. Puerto Vallarta in 1963 was still undeveloped, and Mismaloya, nine miles away, was primitive. It would all change after the movie wrapped because of the enormous publicity the film brought to the area. But when they went down, housing was still being built for the cast and crew.

"The press gathered down there," Huston told me, "expecting something to happen with all these volatile personalities being there. They felt the lid would blow off and there would be fireworks. When there weren't any, they were reduced to writing about Puerto Vallarta. And, I'm afraid, that was the beginning of its popularity, which was a mixed blessing. The beaches became lined by big hotels and condominiums. The natives have become waiters, chambermaids, or cops. There are traffic jams, burglaries, muggings. Most of the shops are tourist-oriented. None of that was there before we went there."

"It was a fishbowl all right," Ava said. "We were all exposed to the world press. And John was having a ball with it; he was enjoying the whole thing. Elizabeth was a darling because she took a lot off my shoulders. I'm not very good with the press. I'm frightened of them. So I tend to be shy in their presence. And they were all there because of all the situations and relationships. And we were cornered, day and night. Elizabeth was marvelous because she was around the whole time and she was very good with them. Very brave, wonderful, and strong."

Ray Stark recalled the time when the San Francisco journalist Herb Caen came down to write a column. They were all sitting at a bar having drinks when Caen asked them, "If you had one choice as a way of life, what would you want?" One by one, they answered. "Peace," said Stark. "Adventure," said Burton. "Wealth," answered Taylor. "Happiness," chimed Kerr. "Success," said Viertel. "Health," was Ava's choice. Huston one-upped them all when he said, "Interest." As Stark later said, "If you have interest in life, it doesn't matter if you're broke, unknown, unhappy, not at peace, because you can survive. You can have a terminal illness, but if you have interest it keeps you going."

Stark loved all the publicity the film was generating. "It was one of the most publicized pictures of its time," he said. "And Ava was the most popular single lady in that part of Mexico. Every eligible Mexican was after her."

Huston, anticipating fireworks himself, and puckishly eager to stir the pot, had a small gift made for

Burton, Taylor, Kerr, Lyon, Ray Stark and Ava which he gave them before the first afternoon rehearsal. "He passed out these fabulous small pistols, with each bullet engraved with our names," Ava recalled. "Oh, John was a naughty boy, he really was. I put mine away in my purse because I don't like guns. Not even little ones."

"The opportunity for shoot-outs was even greater than those names might indicate," Huston said. "Peter Viertel, before his marriage to Deborah, had had a romantic encounter with Ava. Liz's number-two husband, Michael Wilding, made sporadic appearances as Burton's agent. Tennessee was there with his current lover, and Sue Lyon's intended, a tall, pale youth ravaged by love, haunted the surrounding flora. Word got out that he was murderously inclined toward both Burton and Skip Ward, who had love scenes with Sue." To add to the tensions, Huston brought in Emilio Fernandez as an assistant director. Fernandez once shot a producer in the leg over some disagreement, and rumors would swirl around him and Ava that made for romantic speculation in the press.

The craziness that did occur happened off screen, not on. Tommy Shaw, Huston's first AD, fell twenty feet and broke his back when his balcony collapsed. Sue Lyon's boyfriend was barred from the set to keep him from making out with Lyon in front of everyone. Tennessee Williams berated the shit out of one of the Mexican bartenders on several occasions. Larry Tarr, Bappie's husband, came down as a photographer, got drunk and wound up in jail. "Ray Stark came to tell me, 'Your brother-in-law's in a Mexican jail,'" Ava said. "Not a very safe place to be. He's in there with drug addicts and killers; they've got knives and guns. Larry's a nice man but when he gets drunk, you can't stop him; he goes wild. He was crazy on tequila as everybody else was and I don't know what he did or how the police caught him but he wound up in the pokey. We finally got him out of there and put him on a plane and sent him back to New York. But my God, the drinking that went on down there!"

It was Richard Burton who suggested to Huston that they should have a few open bars on the set. Huston thought it a wonderful idea. "The minute you got to work," Ava said, "the first thing you bumped into was the bar. And that was before you had to walk up the hill to the make-up and all that jazz."

Getting to work was part of Ava's exercise routine. She water-skied behind a speedboat every morning. She was staying in a house that had a wall around it and no roof. The young Mexicans who played the beach boys who followed her around in the movie were always "high on pot," she laughed. "They were also high from this thing called *raicilla*, which is like tequila, only it twists your mind, and those cats were on that. They were always lying all over the beach. I'd wake up in the morning and two or three of these beach boys had scaled my wall like monkeys and they'd be out cold in the middle of the patio, next to my bedroom. I had to sober them up, so they could run the boat to get me to work. And once there we had to walk or take a jeep to get up and down the hill because there were no roads. You were exhausted before you got there. It was really wild. John spent as much time arranging where people lived, who was to be there and who was with whom, and how we'd all get to the set, as he did on the script. But he had a really good time. And I'll say this: he creates a whole atmosphere, not just with the actors but the whole set. I've worked with some damn good directors that I liked a lot and leaned on them a hell of a lot, because I felt I needed that. Each director has his own method of getting what he can out of actors. But John is unique. I relied completely on him. There was no doubt in my mind. He had my complete trust."

Though their initial encounter seventeen years earlier left her wet and out of breath, Ava had come to appreciate Huston as a dear friend and perhaps even a genius in his own way.

"You can't compare him to anybody," she said. "Whether you were an intellectual or a nitwit, John had so many sides to be with them. Somebody else like John is Robert Graves—both had time for everyone, except phonies. Each would absolutely annihilate phonies, but never would they pick on somebody not their own size. Like Noel Coward, who would do the same thing. But never to somebody who couldn't protect himself. But I see a lot of similarities between John and Robert Graves. Both very noble men and wonderful friends. It didn't matter if you were a jockey or a lousy actress, as I am, and I'm certainly not an intellectual—John had a way of directing that was quite amazing. A really fine, intelligent actor like Richard Burton, he could talk to. But with somebody like me, I don't know what he does, but it's pure magic. He puts you in the mood and then lets you go. He doesn't tell you what to do, but he gets you in such a situation that you do the right thing."

The example she gave was when she was supposed to go into the ocean wearing a bikini with the beach boys following her. "God knows what hanky-panky is supposed to be going on between them," she said. But it didn't feel right and she couldn't bring herself to do it. "When I get frightened—like I am with that recorder sitting on the floor—I completely close up. In the scene in *Iguana*: I had this mental thing about it. I said, "John, I can't do it, not in the daytime. If it were at night it wouldn't be so difficult." He had lights brought in from Mexico City. He went through God knows what sort of trouble and lost a whole day's work, but he literally turned the day scene into a night scene. I was still frightened. He went in the water with me, holding my hand. No bikini. He said, 'Wear the same old raggedy thing you've been wearing, it's more plausible anyway, she wouldn't stop to undress and put on a bathing suit. She just goes in.' So he waded in the water with me and stayed with me, not saying a word, until I was ready and he said, 'All right, Kid.' And we did the scene in one take. That was the magic of the man when he directed."

Just as she felt so positive about Huston as a director, she felt that playing off Richard Burton as an actor was as good as it gets. "I never worked with anybody who gave so much in every scene," Ava marveled. "He was like a great tennis player. When he hits the ball back, you get something from him. And he makes you laugh and cry. You watch those wonderful eyes and listen to him. So good. And the next day what you see on the screen, though still great, is just half of what he really is. It's funny that the camera does not pick up the greatness of Richard."

They were filming on Nov. 22, 1963, three days after Tommy Shaw had broken his back, when Ray Stark brought news of President Kennedy's assassination. "Ray had this boat offshore where they could send for things we needed, like my bras. He had ship to shore communication. Everybody knew my bra size. And that's how he heard what had happened to Kennedy. We were on our way home for lunch and you have never seen so many drunks sober up so quickly. It was like a total black curtain came down. It was a dreadful time. Everyone was in tears. Even the Mexican kids. I met Kennedy once and he was so charming. We lost a great president. And probably a lot of others too, who wouldn't bother running, because who the hell wants to have their brains blown out?"

The depression that set in among the cast and crew had already reached Tennessee Williams, who had already begun his downward spiral after the death of his former lover Frank Merlo that year. Williams referred to the sixties as his "stoned age." In his 1975 *Memoirs* he tried to chronicle his "collapse" in that decade, drugged up from pills and liquor to the point where he felt "too bizarre in my behavior...for even the conservative members of the gay world." What was of interest to me was that he never wrote about his time with Huston and the movie crew in Mexico.

"God, I adored him," Ava said about the playwright. "He was marvelous. He disagreed with the ending. But I thought John was absolutely right." Williams saw Burton's character as a broken man, destroyed in the end by Ava's domineering, forceful character. Huston saw it differently. Ava played Maxine as more nurturing than Bette Davis had on Broadway, and he felt that she could offer the Reverend Shannon redemption. "John asked Tennessee to think it over. Basically you were seeing the relationship between a man and a woman the way John saw it. John said to Tennessee, 'Listen, you are a homosexual and I know you disagree with this ending, because you don't want to see a man and a woman in a loving relationship.' And Tennessee didn't want to hear that at all."

"He wanted her to be a female spider," Huston told me. "He had written her sympathetically, but he was pulling back his sympathy at the end. But to me the most amusing character was the one played by Ava Gardner, who had the most penetrating remarks. Tennessee's problem was that he had it in for women."

"Tennessee was there the whole time," Ava recalled. "He was there with a great friend of his, this old lady; I don't know her name [Marion Vaccaro]. They were quite funny. He told us that they were once walking down the street in New York and this very skinny girl walked by and Tennessee said, 'God, there goes anorexia if I ever saw it.' And his lady friend said, 'Oh stop it. You know everybody, don't you?' Isn't that hilarious?"

The thought of a woman named Anorexia cracked her up. She needed to finish her wine and light another cigarette before she continued. "I went with this lady and Tennessee to a little restaurant on the beach where we were meeting John and the others. When we arrived, there weren't enough chairs; we were one short for the lady. Tennessee was in his cups and he was furious. He insisted that we leave, which we did. The owner was angry that he had lost us because John hadn't arranged for that extra chair. But Tennessee was so pissed at John. Didn't take much to make him angry. And he never agreed with the ending."

"I met him once," I mentioned. "It was after my interview with Marlon Brando had come out and I was asked to talk about it on TV. The guest before me was Tennessee Williams, and after he was done I approached him and invited him to dinner with me and Marlon. I hadn't spoken to Marlon about it, I was just winging it. I figured if I called Brando and said I was with Tennessee that he might join us. But Williams had a plane to catch, so I couldn't pull that off."

"He's so fat now," Ava said of Brando. "He was so handsome. I don't much care for method actors, but he was the greatest of them. How the hell did he get so good? But he's a strange man. The first time I met him was in the late forties, before he was an enormous star. I had come out of makeup and he was leaning against a car. He said 'Hi.' I said 'Hi.' I wasn't quite sure who he was. He said 'What's your name?' I said 'Ava.' He said, 'Oh, okay.' And that was the end of our conversation. Then years later when I was in New York he telephoned me and asked me out. I had a hangover, so I told him no. Then I felt dreadful because I would have liked to meet him. He called again a couple of days later and asked if I'd like to go see a film with him. So he picked me up at my hotel and we walked to this place where he had booked a room to show some film about the Indian situation. 'Perhaps you could help me with this,' he said. I told him that I was useless when it came to making speeches or doing helpful things like that. There was another film being shown when we got there and we had to wait. We sat there for half an hour—he didn't complain—and then we went in and saw this film about the famine and misery and poverty of the Indians. Then we went back to his hotel near Central Park and the place was crawling with Indians, all in sari's. India Indians. We sat on the floor and had some drinks. I wasn't wearing a bra and all of a sudden he reached over and grabbed my breasts and asked, 'Are those real?' I said, 'I believe they are.' It was completely impersonal, like a doctor. He intended to shock me—and he did. And that was my experience with Marlon Brando."

"Do you ever watch his films on TV?"

"I love to watch movies on TV. I laugh, I cry, I'm still affected by them. I saw *Apocalypse Now* on TV just the other day—just caught the end of it when he was going mad, but I turned it off when it got to the killing of the animals. I can't watch that. I also saw *Night of the Iguana* recently. When I first saw it as a movie I thought I was pretty good. I was so involved with it, I enjoyed it, and I very seldom enjoyed working. But seeing it twenty years later on TV, I was embarrassed. I saw another dimension of Richard, who was amazing, and how extremely good Deborah was. But I found mine lacking."

Lacking, as in judgment, might be the best way to describe Ava's agreeing to play Sarah, the mother of the Jews, in Huston's next picture, *The Bible*. Billed by producer Dino De Laurentiis as "the most important movie of all time," it was far from that. Originally conceived as using five directors for a film that would run twelve hours over two days, it boiled down to Huston directing the episodes that people expected when thinking of the Bible: the Creation, Adam and Eve, Cain and Abel, Noah's Ark, Sarah and Abraham, the Tower of Babel, Sodom and Gomorrah.

'I didn't want to do it," Ava said. "The script John gave me had all these archaic words in it. 'I want thee to go forth,' 'Thou art blah blah blah.' What the hell was that? I wasn't the right gal for that. But John, being John, just used that soothing voice of his and convinced me to go along. 'Sure you can do it, honey. Sure you can.' Well, welcome to my new nightmare."

Ava was never happy about *The Bible* and suspected that Huston wasn't either. Besides directing, he also played Noah and was the voice of God. If she caught it on TV she would begin to shake. All because of the man who played her husband, George C. Scott, who fell wildly, passionately, and violently in love with her. Scott became a movie star early, but even before that, he had established a reputation for throwing temper tantrums. His heavy drinking and short fuse brought him the sobriquet "The Wild Man of Broadway," after he opened an artery by punching his hand through a mirror, tearing apart his dressing room and breaking three knuckles in frustration over a personality conflict with a costar in Joseph Papp's off-Broadway production of *Richard III*. But his acting was so powerful and often so chilling that studios and directors were willing to forgive him his indiscretions as long as he could deliver the goods when portraying the volatile, half-cocked WWII General George S. Patton in *Patton*, the impulsive, wise-ass reactionary General Buck Turgidson in *Dr. Strangelove*, or the menacing loan shark Bert in *The Hustler*. He also electrified Broadway audiences in such plays as *Desire Under the Elms, The Little Foxes, Plaza Suite, Uncle Vanya*, and *Death of a Salesman*.

He had refused to accept the Oscar he won for *Patton*, thought happiness wasn't "a particularly attainable state and if it is, I'm not so sure that it's particularly desirable," and felt "disgusted with the lack of personal courage in myself. You try to be a better person and courage is at the core of being a better person."

It took courage to take on Ava when they met in Italy. But it took a better man than he was to treat her the way she deserved.

"I don't like talking about him because it makes me so sad, and it brings back such awful memories," Ava said when I brought him up. "I dealt with men who had tempers, and who could get violent—Lord knows how I had to defend myself against Howard Hughes and Frank Sinatra, and from Artie Shaw's verbal abuse. But George was a different category of animal when he got drunk. When he drank—which was often—look out!"

"Was he in love with you?"

"He said he was. When he was loaded he'd break into my hotel room, which he did in Italy, London and at the Beverly Hills Hotel, attack me to where I was frightened for my life, and scream 'Why won't you marry me?' Well, for one, he was already married, to his third wife, Colleen Dewhurst. And though I would do my best to calm his rage, I would never marry a man who couldn't control his liquor. Me, I'm a happy drunk. I laugh, I dance. I certainly don't break bottles and threaten to kill."

"Scott did that?"

"He did to my poor Reenie when he broke into the Savoy Hotel where I was hiding in the bathroom. He put a broken bottle to her neck asking where I was. And he did it to me as well in L.A."

"Did you think of calling the police?"

"After Reenie and I managed to escape, we called the hotel security and they took him away. He wound up smashing his own room to pieces and the police came and put him in a cell for the night. I think they fined him a pound and sent him on his way."

"How'd you meet him?"

"My dear John Huston. He thought it a good idea to cast me as Sarah in *The Bible*. Scott was his Abraham. So he brought us together one evening before we started shooting and we hit it off. I liked him—a big brute of a man with a crooked nose, but charming. I just didn't know what he'd turn into after a few drinks. Then he lost all his charm and was just a brute."

"Did he actually attack you on *The Bible*?"

"He was a very jealous man, I discovered. If I even mentioned Frank Sinatra's name he would boil over. Talk about possessive! And I had only just met him. I mean, we were together for a few weeks once we started filming, but really, his rages were terrifying. Before shooting one scene he threw a fit, tore off his costume, ripped it to shreds and stormed off the set. I had no idea why. And Huston just sat there saying he would be fine once he calmed down. Sure enough, he was. But that kind of behavior just doesn't cut it with me."

"When did he throw his first punch?"

"Oh honey, why do you want to go there? It's so dark and ugly." Ava lit a cigarette and blew out a long stream of smoke. She didn't like to kiss and tell. And I was asking her these very personal questions within hours of meeting her. I knew it wasn't polite of me, but I also knew that this was probably my only chance to talk to her about these movies she made for Huston. John had already told me about Scott's boorish behavior and how he once jumped on his back to keep him away from Ava. "It was me and six others," Huston said. "I didn't much care for Scott after that, but a man drunk and in love behaves with a degree of madness sometimes." Huston hired some goons to follow and protect her from him after that. But I wanted to hear it from her, to confirm what Huston had said, and to get it from her perspective. So, I waited, not answering her.

"Well, it boiled over at this small hotel in Avezzano," she said. "We had gone out for dinner, and when we returned, we went back to his room for a few more drinks. Big mistake. I don't remember what we said that got him so enraged, but I saw how he changed, how his eyes narrowed and reddened, how his jaw clenched. When I got up to leave he leaped up and threw a punch, he hit me in my face. I backed away and he came after me, showering me with his fists.

I was so shocked I didn't know what to do. I wasn't expecting this from him. And I was trapped in that room as he beat me for God knows how long, until I managed to escape. And the next day on the set, the makeup man was in shock. He couldn't hide all the bruises. Everybody on the set who saw me knew what had happened. Huston was furious, but he wouldn't let me quit. So I had to do my scenes with George."

Before I saw Ava I had talked to Zoe Sallis, who played Ava's handmaiden in *The Bible*, and was John's mistress and the mother of their son Danny. And I had interviewed Tom Shaw, John's Assistant Director. Sallis said that "George was crazy about Ava and she seemed like she was crazy about him, then she'd turn off. Ava's got a sort of madness and she attracts mad situations, drama, passion."

Tom Shaw told me how he was always separating George and Ava. "Two drunk people don't make for a good love affair," he said. "I'm almost convinced he never fucked her. I don't know why. But they were always loaded...and it was going on constantly." Shaw remembered when Frank Sinatra called him at 3:00 A.M. "He wanted to know if it was true what he heard: that George Scott beat the shit out of Ava." Shaw lied and said he hadn't because he didn't want to get between Scott and Sinatra.

"What did George say to you?" I asked Ava about the incident in Avezzano. "Did he even remember hitting you?"

"Oh, he only had to look at me to remember what he did. My face was swollen like a balloon. And he was apologetic, ashamed, promising it would never happen again. But that's what drunken bullies always say. And never mean."

"Is this when John hired protection for you?"

"Yes, they appeared when we went to Sicily. Three big guys who were always around, but kept their distance. Until one night when George and I were having dinner in Taormina. Don't ask me why I was having dinner again with him, but that's the way it was with me. I was always ready to forgive. I felt sorry for him. George had a few drinks too many and was starting to make a scene—he didn't care where we were when he got this way—and these three guys came to our table and escorted him away. He actually wound up in the nuthouse with bars on the window. John would send me to get him out so we could finish the picture. They had to give him injections when he went crazy to calm him down. He'd stay in the nuthouse for two or three days, have his withdrawals, and then John would say, 'All right honey, would you go and get George?' Reenie would say to me, 'Miss G, don't go there to that fucking crazy man, he'll kill you.' I'd get him out of the nuthouse and we'd start all over again, and then he'd drink again. When George was sober he was highly intelligent, and God knows a wonderful actor, but when he drank he became crazy and beat women."

"Was that the end of you and George?"

"Ha! I wish. But no. After the movie wrapped I went to London to see my dear friend Robert Graves. He was giving a lecture at Oxford. I checked into the Savoy Hotel and who winds up there as well but George. He had followed me to London. Insisted we have dinner. Promised he would control himself. So, we had dinner. And he had too many drinks. Again. So I got out of there as fast as I could. That's the time he chased me back to my room, where I hid in the bathroom and he broke the door down and took the broken bottle to Reenie's neck. We both managed to escape through the bathroom window and he wound up spending the night in jail."

"Goodbye George C. Scott. And good riddance!" I said.

"Not quite. There was one more incident to come, and that was the worst of all. I was in L.A. staying in a bungalow at the Beverly Hills Hotel. George somehow found out where I was and he didn't bother calling, he just came around to the back of the bungalow sometime after midnight, broke the glass window and forced his way in. He was completely drunk and out of his mind. Kept saying he wanted to marry me, and if I didn't marry him he would kill me. He knocked me down, then pinned me down and kept hitting me. I almost lost consciousness, but somehow I managed to keep talking to him. He smashed a bottle—the man liked to smash bottles—and waved the jagged glass at my face. I thought this time it was all over for me. He was going to destroy me right there on the floor. 'Let me call a doctor,' I said to him, repressing the screams that I knew would cause him to cut me. All I could do was say, 'George, George, it'll be all right, you just need some help. Let me help you.' Of course I wanted to help him to keep him from pounding on me. He refused and kept threatening me, but finally he got worn down and I called my doctor to give him an injection so he could be peacefully removed from the premises. And let me tell you, *that* wasn't easy. Jesus, that was a scary time. Probably the scariest time."

I didn't tell Ava then that I had interviewed Scott for *Playboy* in 1980. He was a tough interview until he had a few drinks, and when we met at his house in Greenwich, Connecticut, he drank a full pitcher of Bloody Marys. In the twenty hours that I spent taping him over five days he went through a gamut of emotions as we covered his acting career, his secret writings, his right-wing politics, and his self-analysis. "Acting," he told me, "rescued me from myself. I have a lot of self-hatred." But he also said that he "loved fucking around. I'm so tired of being looked upon as some dreary sicko." He cut me off though when I brought up Ava's name. "I never talk about Ava," he said. "That was a very, very low point in my life. Don't ask me *anything* about her."

■ ■ ■

I attempted to joke with her that it seems like she drove men crazy. "Oh God, no!" she said. "It was never me. It was the alcohol. Especially with Scott. He couldn't handle it."

But it wasn't just Scott. It was Mickey Rooney and Howard Hughes and Artie Shaw and Frank Sinatra and most of the men who caught a whiff of Ava and became intoxicated. And when they couldn't make her their own they lashed out. And yet, somehow she survived. She moved to Spain and then to London. She kept them all at a distance, except when she wanted to let them in. She would tell me about some of them when I would see her again in 1988, when she came to Los Angeles to be treated for a partial stroke.

We had covered most of what I had come to talk about with her, though I did want to ask her about the cameo appearance she made at the end of *The Life and Times of Judge Roy Bean*. Paul Newman played the corrupt, flamboyant judge, who built this town named Langtry in honor of the woman he worshipped but had never met, the performer Lillie Langtry. She finally shows up stepping off a train, and is greeted by Billy Pearson, Huston's great friend, who wasn't an actor but a jockey. Huston thought it would be funny to have him be the one who greets the beautiful Miss Langtry. And since it wasn't a speaking part, Pearson decided he could say anything he wanted to her, as it wouldn't be in the movie anyway.

Ava, who was 50 at the time, was Huston's choice for Langtry because he believed it to be perfect casting. Victoria Principal and Jacqueline Bisset were also in the film and Principal remembered that when Ava arrived in Tucson, "She didn't walk into the room; she came in like a cat. I had never seen a woman move like that or have that kind of presence, before or since. I've never seen a woman electrify a room sexually like she did. You were aware that she was on the prowl." John Milius, who wrote the screenplay, recalled that soon after Ava arrived "she got drunk and got angry at everybody, broke some glasses and stormed off into the desert."

George C. Scott was also in Tucson at the time, working on a different film. When Huston got wind of this he hired a bodyguard for Ava, making sure the man stayed outside her hotel room door throughout the night.

Pearson, who had told me about some of the great pranks he and Huston had pulled off over the years, sparkled when he related what he said to Ava while the cameras rolled. "I wanted to fuck it up," he said. "I knew I was the only guy in the living world who could have done it, because everybody else there was serious in the motion picture business and I just did it as a joke. So when John called 'Action!' and they take ten minutes to get the train coming in just as the sun was going down, I knew it would be impossible to get this antique train to stop on cue a second time. And Ava Gardner didn't know me from Adam. So when she got off the train, I said, 'Well, Miss Langtry, you don't know how nice it is to see you. All I can think about is eatin' your pussy!' None of this, of course, was going to be in the movie. And she said, 'Oh, really?' So I said, 'Me and my buddy here have been out here so long, all we do is jack off dreamin' about ya.' And she just goes right ahead saying her lines exactly as if what I had said was what I was supposed to have said. She was such a professional. I could not shock her. When we came to the end of the thing where we're starting down the stairs, people were rolling. John was wiping tears from his eyes. The producer was a basket case, because if they had to keep Ava another day he had to buy her a Mercedes as a penalty. And of course it all had to be shot again. It would have been the end of me if John and I hadn't been buddies."

"I'm sure John put him up to it," Ava said, reminded of that time. "That little jockey wasn't an actor, but he was quite a character. He kept trying to get me to break character. The two of them were quite a pair, a regular Mutt & Jeff."

"Any opinion of Paul Newman?" I wondered.

"Yes," she said. "One of my unfavorite actors. I can't stand that man. He's an egomaniac. And he's so false. He's on all the time. He's the kind of typical actor that I dislike."

When it was time for me to leave her apartment in London she suggested we take Morgan for a walk by the Holy Brompton Trinity Anglican Church. "I like living here," she said, "because no one bothers me. I had to leave the States because it was just too much. All those journalists, all those stories. God, that's one group of people I cannot bear."

"Was there any particular story that did you in?" I asked.

"There have been so many lies and ugly stuff. That whole thing with *Confidential* magazine," she said. "Do you know about that? That was particularly hurtful. It was like a thousand years ago."

I knew what I had read about it. It had to do with an affair she supposedly had with Sammy Davis Jr. They had published some pictures of the two of them....

"We found out that Sammy had something to do with that. Publicity, you see. Probably didn't do him any harm to be linked with me. God knows everyone else seemed to be at one time or another."

"You mean Sammy set you up?"

"Well, let's say that he was involved. He gave presents to the journalist, gold cufflinks. He supplied the photographs of us when we were sitting around casually, saying that they were made in his apartment."

"Where were they made?"

"In my hotel in New York. Sammy was Frank's friend. He stood by Frank when he was down. He gave me gold earrings for my wedding with the initials A.S. for Ava Sinatra. So when he asked if I'd pose with him for a Christmas cover of *Ebony*, I said sure. He came to my hotel with an entourage, they covered a wall with red paper, I wore a red dress, he dressed as Santa Claus, and we took pictures. In some he sat on the arm of my chair, his arm around back. Next thing I know, we're being linked as secret lovers, and I'm sneaking off to Harlem to fuck him. That's what Frank's friend did."

"How did you find out that he did this?"

"Howard Hughes had a man working for *Confidential*, because Howard was one of their first victims. Howard had his ways, you know. So I knew what was coming before it first came out."

"Did you try and stop them from publishing the photos and writing what they did?"

"I wanted to. I went to Metro about it, got their lawyers involved, but Howard Strickling, Metro's head of publicity, said, 'Don't. If you sue, you can only lose, because you can't stop it and you'll only create bigger headlines when you start suing. And if you win, you win nothing.' *Confidential* was a rag at that time, it wasn't particularly popular. Howard thought they operated out of a cellar. 'You will give them exactly what they want,' he said. 'Publicity. And you get nothing, except maybe a retraction which nobody reads. And all the lies they print will be reprinted in all the newspapers, so you lose.' And that's why I've never sued. I've never attempted to. Because you can only lose. Look at Frank, with the great power that Frank has, with all his good lawyers. When he tried to sue that bitch who wrote that book about him [Kitty Kelly] all he did was give her great publicity. That book became a tremendous seller. On the other hand, I think it made a lot of friends for Frank because a lot of people were incensed about it, people who didn't particularly like him. His records started selling like mad again. And the press suddenly turned to his side. So actually she really hasn't done any damage."

"Guess Howard Strickling's advice wasn't that good," I said.

"Oh, there are an awful lot of people, darling, who love to believe. Including people you wouldn't think would be so gullible. My sister, for one. Bappie will read something to me from the *Enquirer* and when I protest she will say, 'Where there's smoke there's fire.' And this is after all the lies printed about me over the years! And when I tell her she's reading lies and shit, she gets furious with me. Really angry. When all that stuff was going on between Frank and that awful bitch writer, she went and got her book and would read it every fucking day. I'd say, 'Bappie, why are you reading that?' And she'd say the bitch had said some nice things about me, or at least some truths. But I saw that bitch on television talking about the facts in the book, and these are not facts, for fuck's sake."

"Have you read it?"

"I won't. I refuse to." And then, as if talking about the press conjured them up, she nodded in the direction of a few tall trees and whispered, "There are two cameramen with long lenses hiding in the trees."

After we had circled the church and neared her apartment she invited me to play tennis with her the next day. Tennis with Ava Gardner! I couldn't think of a more enticing invitation. But there was a problem: I was in London to interview dozens of people for my Huston book and had lined up two or three interviews each day. I was scheduled to see the writer Edna O'Brien the next day at the time Ava wanted to play. O'Brien had been a difficult person to land, as she had had a lot of problems working with Huston on a project that never made it to the screen. "Maybe another time," I said to Ava, with a great deal of sorrow.

"Yes, of course," she said. "You're busy, I can see. Well, you have my number. You can always call."

Two years later, when I was home in Los Angeles working on my book, my phone rang. It was Ava. "I have a proposition," she said.

2

"Before I Die"

SHE WAS CALLING FROM LONDON.

"How is your book coming along?" she asked.

"It's coming," I said. "I didn't start writing until John died. If he hadn't, I'd still be talking to him."

"Such a wonderful man. He lived quite a life."

"He lived quite *a lot* of lives," I said.

"Yes he did."

"Like you, I suspect."

"Oh I don't know about that. I was always afraid. Dear John had no fear."

"Except of his mother."

"Really? See, I didn't know that. The things you find out. But I'm sure if John chose you he's in good hands."

And then she got to the reason for her call. "I'm going to finally write my book," she said. "You know, they've been after me for years."

"I'm sure."

"Well, I guess it's time, before I die. You know I haven't been well."

43

"I'm sorry."

"Damn nuisance. But we can talk about that later. I'm going to be in L.A. and I thought we might get together when I'm there. I'd like you to work with me on the book."

This took me by surprise. I had only met Ava that one afternoon when we shared some wine, ate a few quail eggs, walked her dog around the park and talked about John Huston.

"You're wondering why you?" she asked, responding to the pause in conversation from my side.

"Actually, yes."

"Well my dear, I just figured if you're good enough for John Huston, you're damn well good enough for me."

I didn't know what to say to her. I didn't want to say that I had only written the first seven chapters of the Huston book and had twenty-four chapters to write. This was Ava Gardner calling. You don't make excuses to *not* see Ava Gardner. "Ava, I look forward to seeing you," I said.

"And I you, darling. Jess Morgan will be in touch."

Morgan was her business manager. I knew him slightly because he was also John Huston's business manager. He called a few days later to tell me when Ava was coming, where she would be staying, and that even though I was working on the Huston book, I should take advantage of this opportunity and meet with Ava at least on the weekends. "She's had a stroke," he said, "and who knows how long she's got.

If she's ready to talk, you should just go and let her talk. Then we'll see where it goes."

Before I arrived at the Westwood Marquis on Saturday, January 23, 1988, I stopped at At-Ease, a men's clothing store in Westwood, and bought a tweed sports jacket for $350. It was an extravagance because I rarely wore sports jackets, but I just felt I needed to dress up for Ava, who was registered at the hotel under the name Ann Clark. I had mentioned to Al Pacino that I couldn't see him that weekend (we usually played paddle tennis and had lunch on Sundays) because my time was now divided between Huston and Ava. "She's worth more than John Huston," Pacino said.

Pacino had once told me that a famous older movie star had once come on to him but he would never reveal who it was. It was always a game with him, to see if I could guess. It could have been anyone—Bette Davis, Jennifer Jones, Elizabeth Taylor, Vivien Leigh, Shelly Winters, Rita Moreno, Greta Garbo, Ingrid Bergman, Audrey Hepburn, Sophia Loren. But I liked to think it was Ava. And when he made that comment, that she was worth more than Huston, I wondered if he was pushing me in her direction because that's who he would have preferred to hear stories about.

"That bag," she said as soon as I walked through the door of her hotel room. "We'll have to do something about *that*."

"What's wrong with my bag?" I asked. It was a Danish school bag—a bit worn, but had lots of pockets and compartments. I had used it when I went to see Marlon Brando in Tahiti, when I interviewed Barbra Streisand, Dolly Parton, Henry Fonda....the bag had a history. No one had ever mentioned it, probably never noticed it. Except Ava.

"My dear boy," she said. "If you're going to be with me you must have something better than that. I'll find you a Gucci bag."

I didn't want to get off on the wrong foot with her, but a Gucci bag? Really? Wasn't it enough that I was wearing a new tweed sports coat?

"You're looking good," I lied.

"Oh please, can the flattery. We must be honest with each other. I look like shit. It's the worst period of my life. Can't move my fucking arm—I'd like to cut the damn thing off. I'm barely alive since I had my stroke."

"You could fool me," I said. "Just that you flew here, that's a long flight for…"

"Someone in my condition? Yes, it was. But they tell me I have a better chance of recovery working with my doctors here."

"How serious has it been?" I asked.

She proceeded to tell me, how it had started the previous fall when she got the flu that never went away. "It just kept recurring." But she didn't have normal flu symptoms. Since she practiced yoga she noticed how her breathing had changed. "I did a lot of deep breathing, and I found that when the breath got almost to the bottom, deep, it was like fire—sharp burning in the breathing." She went to her doctor, went through a series of tests and x-rays, but they came up empty. "All those tests and they found nothing. So they said it was the flu because everyone in London had the flu, it was like an epidemic. You'd feel good for a couple of days and then it would come back, and you'd feel like shit."

This went on for months, she said, until finally she went to see a chest specialist who looked at her x-ray and didn't see what was there. "He wasn't very good, because he was staring at double pneumonia, but he couldn't read it." He had come to her flat, with her regular doctor Jeremy and the x-rays, went into her bedroom where she was coughing and feeling the fire in her lungs, put his stethoscope to her chest and told her she had powerful lungs and would never have emphysema. "Well, with all the smoke I've inhaled all my life that was a relief. But that was the only good news I got from him. He couldn't diagnose what was wrong with me, so I called my doctor here in L.A., Bill Smith, and he said if I was up for it, to come see him."

She may not have been up for it, but she decided to fly anyway, sick as she was. And once in the air, her temperature soared as the plane did. "I run a very low normal temperature that runs in our family," she said. "So what's normal for others is already a slight temperature for me." When her temperature reached 103, she knew how high that was, and so did the stewardesses, who saw this world-famous woman about to collapse in her seat. Passengers were asked to move out of the back row and Ava was able to lie down across the three seats. "I never lie down," she said. "But I didn't have a choice. They put some blankets over me and I just wheezed until my head was pounding, my body felt like jelly inside, and I thought, baby, you've made a big mistake getting on this plane. I must have shivered halfway across the Atlantic."

Her sister Bappie was there when she arrived. Bappie had been in touch with St. John's Hospital and they sent someone with an oxygen tank. Ava was hoping to go back to Bappie's house but one look at her and Bappie knew that they had to go directly to St. John's. And that's when a new series of tests began. She was given antibiotics. She was poked with needles and given various drips, but nothing helped. Her temperature went to 105. Out of desperation, one of the doctors ordered 60 milligrams of cortisone and that brought her temperature down. But she wasn't coughing, so all the congestion in her chest wasn't coming up. Ten days later, no longer in the hospital, she had a stroke.

It began just after dinner at Bappie's, with them sitting in the living room. Ava felt a tingling sensation in the palm of her left hand. Then it went to the area around her nose. She had no headache, no pain. Just this strange needles-and-pins feeling which was spreading. They watched a Laurel and Hardy movie on TV and when it was over, with the numbness in her palm now past her elbow, they called Dr. Smith.

He came around midnight and asked Ava to lift her left hand. She did. Then he asked her to close her eyes and touch the tip of her nose. She couldn't. "It was wandering all over the place," she said. "We were laughing. It was like the Laurel and Hardy movie we had just seen. I wasn't in any pain. It was just funny."

Dr. Smith told her to get a good night's sleep but by morning it wasn't so funny. "I woke up and the whole left side was gone. The only thing I could move was my big toe. The leg was gone. The arm was gone—it was literally glued to my body, we almost had to break it to move it. My mouth wasn't working. My speech was slurred. My damn tongue was like it had been injected with Novocain."

And yet…"I wasn't frightened. I wasn't depressed. Which was very strange, but that's the way the brain works, it protects you from the horror of the situation."

She was rushed to St. John's where a physiotherapist began working with her and after a week he managed to get her out of bed. "I couldn't even walk," she said. "But I was laughing all the time. I really was, because it hit my bladder and I was peeing a lot as well.

"They tied this thing around my waist. But this therapist, he was Egyptian and very strong, he had a will of iron, very determined. And he transferred that determination to me. I had to learn to walk—imagine that. Isn't this the biggest bore you ever heard in your whole life?"

For a woman whose life was like a modern day Zorba the Greek, who lived to dance, drink, eat, fuck and just take from life all that was there to grab, talking about being bedridden and bound to a wheelchair and tied around her waist as she relearned how to walk, tongue-tied and half paralyzed was, yes, certainly a bore. But she was still a relatively young woman, in her mid-sixties, and she was—or had always been—a fighter.

"I was fortunate," she said. "I was in great physical condition because I had been on a six-month health kick before this happened. I cut down on smoking. Stopped drinking. Healthy diet. A lot of exercise—tennis, yoga and swimming. I swam every day in this icy water at this little gym a five-minute walk from my house. Even in the wintertime. So my legs were strong, which was a great help."

During her therapy, the Egyptian put his hands on her shoulders and Ava took a few steps. "It was absolutely marvelous!" Within a week, with the help of a three-footed cane, she was walking down the hospital corridor in her bare feet.

"You don't wear slippers?" the Egyptian asked.

"You know," Ava said, "I once did a movie called *The Barefoot Contessa*. When the director, Joe Mankiewicz, came to Rome to ask me to be in it, I told him 'Wonderful. I've got beautiful feet.' And he said, 'Ava, it requires a little bit more than beautiful feet.'"

The Egyptian promised to see that movie. He didn't insist on the slippers.

Ava worked with him for the next two months, taking three steps without the cane, then six, then finally walking outside, at which point she left the hospital and returned to Bappie's. Though her doctors felt she should stay in L.A. to work on her recovery, she was anxious to get back to her flat in London and her dog Morgan. "I knew I'd get better if I was happy where I was, and I'm happy when I'm home in my own surroundings. I wasn't happy in Los Angeles. I had stopped laughing and a terrible blackness came over me. It wasn't gradual, it happened instantly. While I was still at the hospital I felt this dark cloud that wouldn't go away. I recognized it as depression, because it had happened to me once before when I had a hysterectomy twenty years ago. It gave me terrible vertigo and I felt like I was living in an earthquake that never stopped quaking. A woman's body gets all confused after a hysterectomy. So this time I knew what this blackness meant and I knew the fun times were over. They gave me an antidepressant called Elavil, which is a remarkable drug, but it takes about three weeks before it begins to work. The side effects, though, are hell. My face swelled, my moods changed, I felt anxious, pissed off, confused, dizzy, off balance, my vision blurred, and I began having nightmares. And then after a month….the black curtain lifted. So I went home, stayed on Elavil, which is called Tryptizol in England, for six months, and continued therapy for a year until…" She paused and then asked, "Can we talk about something else for a minute? I really am fed up with this story."

"You're angry about it," I said. "But something happened over there that brought you back here."

"There was a setback. London is a very big city, and I had to go from here to there for my therapy. It could take a whole day, just the traveling. So when I felt well enough, I figured I could do it at home."

And then she told me about the trampoline.

Just when she thought she was well enough to be on the road to recovery she got in touch with an organization that helped stroke victims. They sent a young woman to work with her. Because Ava had regained much of her strength, the girl suggested that a small trampoline might be fun for her to try. Ava thought it was a wonderful idea because she was bored from just lifting weights, and she still couldn't do more active sports like tennis. Because she had a stationary bicycle in her bedroom, she thought the best place for the trampoline would be in the living room in front of the fireplace, so she could use her right hand to hold onto the mantel when getting on. Her left hand was still useless. And so was the girl who suggested this, since she wasn't always going to be there when Ava bounced.

"It might have been a fine idea if she were holding onto my hand," Ava said with more than a hint of disgust in her voice. "I mean, darling, when I was in St. John's, they were so careful with me, they wouldn't let me take two steps without someone there next to me. There was always supervision during my therapy. But when I got home and used this organization, it was a different story. I was on my own. My fault, I guess, for going on the damn thing, but hell, why would she have suggested it if it was going to be dangerous?"

"You fell?" I asked.

"Honey, I *crashed*! My hand went, damn it, and I crashed on the marble fireplace, the hearth, and injured my spine quite badly. I heard something crack. I thought for sure I broke my back or my hip."

"Were you alone?"

"Goddamn right I was alone. It was goddamn midnight! Well, my housekeeper Carmen was nearby and I was able to call her. She came and saw me laying there in horrible agony and called my doctor, who came immediately." But instead of calling for an ambulance and taking her to the hospital, he gave her a painkiller and returned in the morning to take her there. An x-ray showed that she had a crushed vertebra. It wasn't as bad as she had feared, but it still meant that her physical therapy would have to be put on hold. She needed three months of bed rest. "That was the worst possible thing when you're trying to rebuild muscles and strength. A tremendous setback!"

"And you blame this girl because she didn't warn you...?"

"I was so fucking mad, honey. And I still am! Anger is a terrible emotion—it eats the hell out of you. But it also keeps you going. And it was the only thing that kept my depression down."

"Were you also angry with yourself for doing this unsupervised?"

"I'm angry that the whole thing happened, how's that? And I don't know who to blame. I'm terribly angry at that girl. For the first time in my life I feel like I want revenge. I would take pleasure in breaking *her* back."

"Did you see her again?"

"Oh, we had an appointment a couple of days after that happened, but she didn't show up. Then, two days later, she came to the door. I was there alone. She asked me how everything was. She didn't know I had fallen. I told her to please go away. I didn't want to see her. She didn't understand, so I told her what happened, and I said, politely, that the trampoline wasn't a very wise decision, and that she should know her patients and their weaknesses. I wish I wasn't so polite, I'm sorry about that. I wish that I had pushed her down the stairs."

The therapy and the recovery continued and some months later she was able to swim again. She wasn't trusted to walk alone, so Carmen walked with her. She was doing leg and arm exercises at the gym. She was still getting cortisone, but it went down from sixty milligrams to one, along with small doses of chemotherapy. "The chemo works with the cortisone," she said. "Otherwise, your system can't take it if you just stop the cortisone." She had injections where they could follow what was going on inside her chest with daily x-rays. But her London doctors made a mistake by not taking an x-ray before they started with the injections. She had her x-rays sent to her doctor in L.A. to be diagnosed and when he compared the latest with one from the year before he saw how much she had improved and he said she no longer needed the injections, the x-rays, the cortisone, or the chemo. And then she got shingles.

"One damn thing after another," she said.

As with her depression, she had experienced this too, twenty years ago when she was waterskiing in Acapulco. "I fell, and water can be pretty hard when you're going 50 mph. I thought I had broken a whole gang of ribs. Went to the doctor, who saw this small blister on my chest and said I had shingles. He gave me some vitamin B-12 and though it was painful, it cleared up in a few weeks."

This time, however, the blisters started to make a belt around her chest. It hurt like hell. And it didn't go away in a few weeks. But she had one bit of encouraging news. She was told that having shingles again meant she would not suffer from another stroke. If it didn't hurt so much she would have laughed. What the hell does anyone know about these things? About shingles and strokes and depression? She knew only how she was feeling. And she felt like hell.

"And then I fell off the loo," she told me. "How much more boring can this get? I went in the bathroom, sat down on the left side and smashed into the wall. I was just lying there on the bathroom floor. So between the shingles, my frozen shoulder, and this, I just about had it. I needed people to dress me. I was in such pain that I had given up. I just wanted to lie in bed and drink brandy."

But she didn't give up. She was here, in America, in Los Angeles. She was still numb on the left side, but her left arm wasn't glued to her body because I was able to help her put on her sweater. Her shingles were gone. Her speech wasn't slurred. And she still had a sense of wonder, as I learned when she told me about the TV shows she watched in the hospital.

There was an Elvis Presley film festival playing and she had once had a chance to meet Presley, "but I was in love with another singer at that time," she said, referring to Sinatra. "But Elvis was very handsome; he had beautiful eyes, and a lovely voice. He must have had some classical training because his breathing and his control and his low notes were magnificent. It must have been his birthday when I was in the hospital because they were running all his films and I saw them every day. He was good, but he sure made a bunch of crap."

She also got her first exposure to porn on TV. "Honey, let me tell you, I was searching the channels and hit channel 3, and I started watching this –I don't know what you call it, a movie? I guess that's what it was. Pornography. I didn't know you could watch it so easily. I mean what if a child was in the hospital clicking on this? I asked the nurse if pornography was allowed on American television and she said no. So I told her to sit down with me and take a look at this. The opening scene was two stark naked people on a boat. The actress—not much of an actress—was on top of the guy and they were fornicating like mad. I didn't believe it. There's a flashback to show she's from a good family, and she's about to be married to a charming man. She says to her father, 'Daddy, I love you.' Then she and her fiancé are at the altar exchanging their vows. And then another flashback where she's doing all this fucking before it returns to the wedding, where she says, 'I do.' So now they're married and you hear her voice as she's walking home alone one night saying, 'Why can't I be happy with this man? I love him. I admire him. But there's this other part of me that wants this thing.' And this thing turns out to be the next shot where instead of going home to him she's in a strip joint with this stark naked stripper gyrating on stage. The girl is sitting by herself at a table and a man comes over, an old lover, and he sits down and asks her what does she want? She says she wants what he's always done, as fast and as quickly and as low as possible. In the next scene she's in bed with two broads and this guy and they're all going at it. Then she goes back to her husband and apologizes, says she's so sorry. And that's the story. Not exactly *Gone With the fucking Wind*."

I didn't visit Ava when she was in the hospital, which she visited regularly during the week. But on the second weekend when I went to see her at the Westwood Marquis she asked if I'd mind taking her to her sister's place. She wanted to do a load of laundry, and had thrown the clothes into a large plastic garbage bag. We got into the elevator together and I suggested that she wait in the lobby while I went to get my car. As I walked through the lobby carrying the garbage bag, I turned to see her standing between the elevator and the entrance to the dining room, where a young newlywed couple was posing for pictures. I turned back, to try to protect her from having her picture taken once the photographer recognized her, but it wasn't necessary.

"Excuse me...ma'am," I heard the photographer say to Ava. "Would you mind moving just a bit? You're in the picture." He was totally concentrating on his job, and Ava Gardner was just an uninvited and unwanted hotel guest.

Ava looked at the young man with the camera, then at the smiling couple next to her. She hesitated for a moment—perhaps reflecting for that second on a thousand other moments before ten thousand other cameras. And then she smiled ever so slightly before stepping out of the picture.

"That was funny," she said when we got into my car. "I've certainly been in enough pictures to last a lifetime, though most of them were posed and cheesecake. I hate it when they snap me from a distance, when they hang in trees or hide behind cars. Who the fuck wants to have to go through life being made up? I've been lucky that I can go a lot of places and not be bothered."

"You were lucky today," I said. "That wedding photographer could have made more today with just that one shot than he will make working that entire wedding, had he known."

"Well, two cheers for his not knowing, then. Thank fucking God for small favors. I'm surprised no one's taken my picture in the hospital. It's been reported that I've been going there, thanks to Bappie."

Her sister, she said, talked to an English reporter who wrote for *The Sun*. He had flown to L.A. to write a story about Ava in the hospital and went to Bappie's house with a bouquet of flowers and started asking her if it was true that Frank Sinatra was paying for Ava's hospital bills. "He was a nice man," Bappie told Ava. "There is no such thing as a nice reporter," Ava responded. "They don't exist. When a goddamn reporter comes to your house you don't say a word, you don't take his flowers, you just close the door and say you're going to call the police." But that's not what Bappie did, and that's how Ava's private woes became public in the English press.

"At least the American press has left you alone," I said, not sure if they actually had. "Maybe it's the dreary weather we've been having lately."

"Oh, I don't think that stops them. I like the rain."

"Must have rained a lot in North Carolina," I said, thinking about Ava's childhood.

"The other night there was a terrific rain," she said. "It was beating on the window at the hospital and it just flooded me with memories of sleeping at the barn with Daddy at night. The barn was full of tobacco leaves that were drying. That lovely tobacco smell."

Ava looked at the thin rain gently hitting the windshield and began to drift off. She was thinking about her daddy, the barn, and the smell of tobacco. "Tell me about your childhood," I urged.

3

The Ground Under Her Toes

"WE WERE POOR," AVA SAID about growing up in North Carolina as we drove to her sister Bappie's house. "But I wasn't aware of it, because everyone else was poor. But it was wonderful, because we were loved."

"So all your early memories are about how wonderful it was?" I asked. The family had lost the 1400 acres her father Jonas and his older brother Ben had bought seven years before Ava was born because they couldn't afford the $14,000 spread out over fourteen years, so they had to move from Grabtown to Brogden to Newport News. Jonas worked in a saw mill, ran a country store, built his own home and a nearby church, grew tobacco, and helped manage a teacher's residence. He was mild mannered and kept to himself, doing the best he could to provide for his family, but it wasn't easy to eke out a living in those years before the Great Depression. Couldn't have been too wonderful for the adults.

"Oh, even though I was the youngest, I got my share of whippings," Ava said. "I was a terrible tomboy. I remember the first time my daddy did more than talk to me. He had never touched me before this, talking was his thing, and that was always worse. It was snowing and I was climbing on some logs. Daddy said, 'Daughter, get off those logs.' I didn't listen; I just was jumping from log to log. He said it again. I ignored him. He said it a third time and then he snatched me by the arm and he gave me a damn good spanking. It was freezing cold so his hands were cold and that hurt worse than anything else, except my feelings. So when we got back to the house I ran into the kitchen to get warm and to tell Momma what Daddy had done. Before I could even finish she just said, 'Your Daddy's right.' And that was the end of that. They never differed when it came to discipline."

There were other youthful incidents which Ava recalled before we reached Bappie's with her bag of laundry. Like stealing watermelons from the neighbors' fields until her Daddy plunked her on his lap and explained to his six-year old daughter what happened to thieves when they got caught. Or when her sister Inez saved her from falling off the roof after she had climbed out an attic window. Or the time she nearly gave her mother and sisters a heart attack when she climbed the water tower and couldn't climb down. Then there were the accidents. When she walked into a hoe her sister Myra was swinging and nearly lost her eye. Or when she was eight and climbed through a broken school window, the jagged glass carving a two-inch T-shaped gash in the back of her leg, leaving a permanent scar. "Miss Mosely, our teacher, had no sympathy, even when she saw me sitting on the ground with the blood gushing from the artery I had torn. When she told my Daddy that I deserved it because I had no business climbing through that broken window, my Daddy got furious with her, because he saw that I wasn't out of danger. He drove me to Smithfield to see a doctor who stitched me up, but a week later I broke all the stitches climbing a tree, so I've got a very ugly, very jagged scar." All these were stories of her overactive tomboyish ways and telling them made her laugh, especially when it came to outsmarting or outplaying some of the boys her age. There was the time when she took her five-year-old nephew Al Creech, the son of Elsie Mae, to the local general store to buy him a bag of marbles, and he immediately lost them in a game to some older boys. Eight-year old Ava, the protector, challenged those boys and won all of Al's marbles back, and then threatened to bloody any of their noses if they tried to get them back again. "Those little shits were scared of me," she said with some glee. "And they should have been. I would have popped them."

Remembering Al triggered a different memory about the Creech side of the family. It helped provide some of the colorful backwoods background which formed Ava's early years. "Elsie Mae married into some crazy people," she said. "Especially when they were drunk, which was most of the time. Old Man Creech was probably the richest man in Johnston County. His brother was Rufus, who owned nine acres that my Daddy farmed. Elsie Mae married his son David. Another son was Barry, who was born on my birthday. And there was James, who was my brother Melvyn's age, very handsome, very intelligent, and very gun-happy. I adored him. But he was a drunkard, like the rest of them, and he wound up shooting his wife in my sister's house. He had married twice before, both wealthy, social broads—they had proper church weddings, and angry divorces. Then James married a poor little country girl, what they called poor white trash down there, and his family was furious about that. Her name was Maddie and they moved to a house on one of his father's farms in Brogden near where Elsie Mae had a little country store. By then her husband David had died and Elsie Mae was running the store by herself, which was fine by her. She had an old potbellied stove in there and all the men in the county came to visit. My sister wound up taking Maddie under her wing because she felt sorry for her, knowing that being married to a Creech was like living in hell. James would go off and leave her for weeks and weeks. This one time he came back from being on a bat for who knows how long and Maddie was staying at Elsie Mae's because she was uncomfortable being at her house alone so long. My other sister Inez and her husband were also there because they were moving from their house in Raleigh over to Smithfield and hadn't chosen a house yet. That night when James finally got home and didn't find Maddie there, he walked over to Elsie Mae's, about five minutes away, and he was drunk, drunk, drunk. When he saw Maddie there he said, 'Elsie Mae, I'm gonna kill her.' And by God, he left and within a few minutes he returned with a shotgun. He was like a wild man. Everyone who was there—Maddie, my two sisters, Inez's husband John, all the kids—ran to the back room and slammed the door. There were no locks on the doors, so John and Maddie were holding the door shut while James was screaming and pounding on it from the other side. When he couldn't push the door open he just blasted away with his shotgun and that's how he killed his wife. The shot went right through her brain. Everyone was screaming and running away, trying to find a place to hide. The kids wound up under the house or behind some bushes. Inez and John saw James walk into the room and shoot Maddie six more times, damn near blew her head off! James was arrested and there was a trial. Not even Old Man Creech, with all his money and his influence, could save James from the electric chair. It was the drink, you see. He was out of his mind, just like the way George C. Scott got with me. With these drunkards, alcohol is sheer poison. They get drunk and become violent and completely crazy. And James wasn't the only crazy Creech. There was his Uncle Johnny who blew his brains out and there was Joe Creech who went hunting and missed a deer and got so mad he blew his own toes off. Wasn't an accident. They were all crazy," Ava laughed. "And that's what Elsie Mae married into."

Ava's childhood was so far removed from my own that I couldn't help marveling that we were from the same country. I grew up on the streets of Brooklyn and in a suburb on Long Island. There were no crazy Creeches, no town drunks, no family members getting shot at, though I did climb our water tower and got my share of whippings. Religion didn't play a significant part of my growing up and I assumed that, too, differentiated my experience from hers, but I was wrong.

"My family were all Baptists," she said. "But religion was not terribly important. There wasn't much going to church—everyone was too busy. I used to go to the church my father built, but that was just for fun, just to go somewhere and take your little penny. My Aunt Ava, my mother's sister, was quite religious. She lived in the house with us when I was a child. She would read the Bible to me all the time. She loved her Bible. But it didn't rub off on me at all. Poor Aunt Ava, nothing she tried with me stuck. She tried to teach me to knit and to sew—that didn't work. She tried to teach me to be a lady and not be such a tomboy and that didn't work. Eventually, she just gave up."

"So," I said, "there was no praying to God when you got stuck at the top of the water tower? Or praying when someone got sick or you wanted something you couldn't have?"

"Oh hell, I don't know about that," Ava said. "Jesus, who remembers those things? It was easier to just cry and get attention that way. But I used to go to the black churches a lot because I loved the way they sang. I'd tag along with Elva Mae, who worked for Momma and was very close to my sister Inez. I'd love how the preacher would rattle the congregation by shouting out what sinners they all were, and I knew I was one because of all the stuff I was learning at school from the older boys, like using cuss words I didn't understand like *fuck* and *shit*, and stealing those watermelons, and smoking tobacco leaves. It was the Holy Rollers all talking in tongues or screaming out to Jesus, people clapping, everybody singing, so wild, so free, so much fun."

Segregation was still a strong part of the South, and with Ava growing into a young beauty, I questioned her about that, feeling certain her parents and sisters must have had some reservations about how easily and innocently she crossed the color line.

"Blacks were part of our family," she said. "I shared a bed with black women when I was a little girl. Big fat loving Virginia was like another mother to me. Every two or three weeks, when Momma went shopping, Virginia would take me to the movies. We'd sit up in the peanut gallery because she couldn't sit down with the whites. So I'd sit there with my blonde tow head among the blacks and we'd have a fine time. We'd take a bag of candy, and afterwards we went to the drugstore for ice cream. And when we'd get home, Virginia and I would act out what we saw in the movie.

"But there were awful things that went on. I never saw a lynching but they happened during my childhood. There was a little boy named Shine who was an orphan. He had no permanent home, but he would show up every summer around the tobacco burning time and Daddy would take care of him. He lived in our house for two or three months. He was one of my favorite chums; I adored him. He had big white teeth and big white eyes and was very black. But when I was about ten or eleven we weren't allowed to play together anymore. That broke my heart and I didn't understand why. I was becoming a young lady, you see, and even though my breasts and my period hadn't appeared yet, my parents decided that it was the time I shouldn't play with Shine anymore."

When her period came, it wasn't her mother she told, but Virginia. "I was twelve and thought I was bleeding to death, even though most of my girlfriends were a year older than me and already had gone through it. But nobody in my family talked to me about it. Sex wasn't discussed at all, where babies come from or any of that jazz. It's unfortunate because those things should be discussed. But in those days, and particularly in my family, it wasn't."

Then Ava had a flashback and started to laugh. "After I learned the word *fuck*, I remember wrestling around with my nephew Al and I got on top of him, pinning him down, and I said, 'Oh Al, let's fuck.' My sister Elsa Mae, Al's mother, heard this and told me about it later. Now, I don't know how in the hell I got to understand about a male and a female on top of one another, but apparently that's what I said. I was lucky, I guess, that nobody washed my mouth with soap or anything, because I grew up with a healthy attitude towards sex."

Just before we arrived at her sister's, Ava told me how Bappie had saved her from flattened breasts. "We were living in Newport News and my little breasts had just started to pop out. I'd done something, sassing Momma in the kitchen, and she started to yell at me. She put up her hand to slap me and then she looked at me and said, 'Young 'un, I'll put a bra on you.' She suddenly realized that I was a young woman and there were breasts there. And my sister Bappie said, 'She is not going to have her breasts ruined by a bad bra.' When she was growing up in the Twenties, it was the Flapper era in which flat breasts were the fashion. My sisters were all big busted girls and Bappie, Inez and Elsa Mae would take straight pieces of cloth and help each other crush their breasts with them and fasten them in back with safety pins. They destroyed their breasts completely when they were young girls. So Bappie said, 'That's not going to happen to Ava. I'm going to bring back special bras from New York for her.' Which she did. I had special little bras when I started wearing them."

Conversations with Ava Gardner

We finally arrived at her sister's house. Bappie had a big but concerned smile when she saw Ava. "Look at that," Ava said as we walked in and passed a small painting on the wall. "Frank did it," she said about a Sinatra still life. Then Ava introduced me by saying that I had been asking her about whether the Gardner family was prejudiced against blacks.

"Oh no, I don't think so," Bappie said earnestly. "To an extent, there was a racial problem. We weren't allowed to play together, but we never had any problems on the farm. We had good Negroes. There was this family, the Browns, and they had a whole gang of kids. We were allowed to go there when Jeanette Brown had a new baby. And when Ava was about three, when we couldn't find her we'd go over to Jeanette's, and there she was, this little thing with a long neck, sitting on the bench having supper with them."

"I was telling Larry about how I used to climb the water tower," Ava said.

"Oh God, you were such a tomboy," Bappie said. "But that water tower thing, that was dangerous. There were some missing planks around the tower, which we didn't know about until Ava climbed up there. Inez was there, I was there, and Momma. There was Ava, by herself, happy as a lark. And we were afraid to say anything, other than 'Ava honey, come on down.' We didn't know what to do. We were practically paralyzed. I expected her to fall right through one of those missing planks. But she sashayed all around that tower until she got tired and then she didn't know how to get down. We sent Melvyn up to get her. Oh, you gave us all a scare that day."

"I climbed like a monkey," Ava said. "I remember there were these crisscrossed poles that I climbed to get up there. I love to climb to this day, if I wasn't so fucking paralyzed."

"You'll recover," Bappie said.

"Not likely, honey," Ava said. "We're not a very long living family. Both our parents died when they were about 57. Daddy died five years before Momma. And Melvin was in his sixties. Inez was 74."

"Elsie Mae was 82," Bappie said about their sister's death the year before.

"Younger than you," Ava noted. "And when did Bobby die?" Bobby was Elsie Mae's son. "He was 37, wasn't he?"

"That was from an accident," Bappie said. "Some of us are still around. You, me, Myra."

Bappie was 84, Ava 65, and Myra 72 in 1988. Beatrice was the oldest of Ava's three sisters. She was 19 and had just gotten married when Ava was born on Christmas Eve, 1922. Elsie Mae was born in 1904, the year after Beatrice, whom Ava called Bappie as a child and the name stuck. Edna Inez was born in 1906. There were also two brothers, Raymond, born in 1909, who died at age two, and Jonas Melvin, whom the girls called Melvin but others called Jack, born in 1911. He was always getting into trouble but would grow up to serve several terms in the North Carolina legislature in the 1970s. The fourth

Gardner daughter, Myra Merritt, came along in 1915, when things started going downhill for the family.

"Larry wants to know about the early years," Ava said as we settled into Bappie's living room. "Before I can remember anything."

For as long as it took to run the washer and dryer, Bappie told me about life in Wilson, Johnston and Smithfield counties at the turn of the 20th century. She spoke about their hard-working, good-natured mother Mollie and her quiet, stately, but naïve father Jonas, who got outfoxed by his brother, Ben. "Uncle Ben was a crook and a womanizer," she said with some bitterness. "He was a disreputable man. My mother couldn't tolerate him. And I disliked him so much. He sold our Daddy out, and he just was never honest with him. He had nine boys who all worked on the farm, while Daddy had all these girls. He was always a bully, to everyone. He wound up in the nuthouse because he was so crazy, but he should have been sent there long before. I never heard anybody say anything nice about Uncle Ben Gardner. He was a selfish, selfish man who pushed my father out of everything."

"I didn't like him either," Ava said. "Didn't he die in a whorehouse?"

"He died from syphilis, which he got in a whorehouse," Bappie said. "Grandma Gardner, his mother, lived with us until I was a big girl, and I remember hearing her say not very good things about Uncle Ben."

There were two other Gardner brothers, Warren and Charlie, but they didn't share in the property Ben and Jonas had mortgaged. "Charlie and Warren had nothing to do with this thing that my father and Uncle Ben did," Bappie said. "They remained in Wilson County when we moved to Johnston County. They were both nice men. Only Ben was disgraceful."

Bappie was two and Elsie Mae a baby when the family moved sixty miles to Johnston County. She remembered going there in a two-horse-drawn surrey with a fringe on top. "Aunt Ava had given me a little porcelain deer. It was my one prized possession and I kept it on my lap in a box filled with cotton because it was so fragile. I was so happy to be going somewhere, but Grandma Gardner was so sad for leaving our home that she started crying, and I remember wondering why Grandma was crying."

They had moved to a big farm where her Daddy operated the saw mill and the gin mill. Uncle Ben lived in the big house, while they lived in a smaller house until Jonas built them a better house with six bedrooms. Ben had a big car, and Jonas was stuck with the horse and buggy until they finally were able to afford a Ford. And when Ben sold the property out from under Jonas, all that was left for Jonas was a small piece of land. Ben got rich. Jonas didn't. "I heard Momma and Aunt Ava and Grandma Gardner talking about what Uncle Ben had done to my father. It was really terrible. And that's when we had to move to Brogden, where they managed the Teacherage. We had school teachers living with us."

"Daddy should have stood up more to Uncle Ben," Ava said. "Maybe that's why I can't stand a bully—and I've faced plenty."

"Daddy wasn't the confrontational kind," Bappie said. "He was such a kind, sweet person...never raised his voice. When we girls would have fights, he would get up, put the newspaper by his side, and parade around the dining room and kitchen where we would be scrambling and say, 'I've seen little boys fight, but I do know I've never seen little ladies fight.' That would get us quiet. He would go to his bedroom and smoke a cheroot, one of those twisted cigars that he liked. But I must say, we paid a hell of a lot more attention to Daddy than we did to Momma."

"Wasn't there a fire?" Ava said. "I remember when I was three and this colored woman was holding me up to the window in our bedroom and outside Daddy's store was burning. That's one of my first memories."

"That was the second big fire," Bappie said. "I wasn't there for that one, but I remember when Melvin burned down the saw mill. Oh, he was one scared young man when that happened. He was maybe seven when he tried to smoke in the seed house, which was a playhouse for us children when there wasn't any seed being stored there. But there was some flammable fertilizer in there when Melvin's cigarette lit the whole place up. Melvin was so scared, he ran out of there and into the house and hid under Momma's bed.

They found him there and dragged him out. He didn't have to go get a switch, they got one for him."

The memory made Bappie laugh, and Ava asked her why she was laughing at such a horrible memory. "I'm laughing about Myra," Bappie said. "She was maybe three when that happened. She had this rabbit that she had begged Daddy for. He was funny about not letting us have pets, but when they were plowing all these rabbits would go scrambling, and there were these little baby rabbits that Myra saw and she wanted one. So Daddy let her have one, which she guarded with her life. She kept it in a box and she just watched it all day, fed it vegetables, checked on it constantly. One day Melvin went to see the rabbit and he let it get away. Myra's heart was broken. She just cried and cried and said, 'I don't know what Melvin's gonna do next. First he burns Poppa's gin and now he lost my rabbit.' She was so sincere, comparing that big fire with the loss of that little rabbit. Oh, that was funny."

What wasn't funny was the death of brother Raymond, which hit the family very hard because it could have been prevented. "I was only seven when it happened," Bappie remembered. "Daddy had been using dynamite to blast stuff on the farm and he kept the explosive caps separate from the dynamite, in a dresser drawer in the bedroom. Early one morning, a few farmers came to get some needed caps. Daddy went and got them. It was in the morning, right after breakfast, just before I was to go to school. Meanwhile, Mother was making her signature cheese biscuits, which were absolutely divine. She would take a bowl of cheese and wrap this dough around the cheese into a ball and bake them in the oven. This particular morning was winter and very cold. Little Raymond was two years, two months and fifteen days old. He was a prize, because he was the only boy, and he was so pretty, such a beauty. He ran in from the dining room for some cheese biscuits, and took them into the bedroom, which had a big open fireplace. After Raymond ran into the bedroom, Momma followed him to sweep up the crumbs and the bark from the burned wood, and dump it all back into the fireplace. What Momma didn't know was that Daddy had dropped one of those explosive caps on the floor. Little Raymond was standing in front of the fireplace when she swept it into the fire. The explosion threw burning wood into his body, in his stomach. Oh, it was a terrible, terrible thing. I was right there. I heard the explosion. Momma grabbed him and ran out to the back porch where there was a big ironing board and she lifted him onto this board to look at him. We didn't have hospitals then, the nearest one was in Raleigh. He was still alive when they got him there, but he didn't survive the night. We were all devastated. Momma was pregnant then with Melvin. She and Daddy were just crushed. Daddy felt guilty for dropping the cap, and Momma felt guilty for sweeping it into the fire. They didn't accuse each other because there was nothing they could do about it. It was just a great tragedy."

Bappie's memories made her tired and once the laundry was done we left. Ava and I continued talking about her childhood in the car, on the way to my house. She wanted to go to Nichols Canyon, where I lived, because she had lived in the canyon in the 1940s and thought it might be fun to see if she could recognize the house. "Bappie never got along with Mickey or with Artie," Ava said, referring to her first two husbands. "But she adored Frank. As a matter of fact, when Frank was trying to prove to me that he wasn't messing around, he stayed up in that Nichols Canyon house with Bappie. But though he might have fooled Bappie, I knew he was still messing around."

We drove up the winding canyon road looking for the house, but Ava wasn't sure which one it was. She remembered making the sharp turn about a mile in, but there were so many more houses that had been built since she had lived there, she just knew the general vicinity. My house was another mile and a half up the canyon and as we zigged and zagged our way there, Ava talked about her brother Melvin, her memory stirred by Bappie's earlier recollections. "I worshipped him," she said. "He was eleven years older, so he was home when I was a little girl. We were very close and I ran all his errands for him, polished his white shoes, learned to iron his shirts. He'd say, 'Sugar, I'll give you a nickel if you will iron this.' I never saw the nickel, but I loved to iron; I found it soothing. That's what I'd do when I'd go into depression, and that's what breaks my heart about this goddamn hand of mine. I can't iron anymore."

My two daughters, five and eight, had a friend visiting when we arrived at my house. Ava was gracious with them as they ran from the living room to their bedrooms and back. She asked them if they had a dog and when they said they didn't, she told them all children should have a dog. "Do you have a backyard?" she asked.

"It's out here," my older daughter Maya said, taking her outside.

"Well, there's certainly enough room for a small dog," Ava said. "Would you like one?"

"Sure," Maya said.

"Then that's done. I will get you a corgi, like the one I have. They're the best dogs. And they don't have a tail. Have you ever seen a dog without a tail?"

"No," Maya said. "Why do dogs need a tail?"

"They don't," Ava laughed. "Except to show when they get excited. But the Queen has corgis. Do you know who the Queen is?"

"Is that the name of your dog?"

"No, my dog is Morgan. But the dog I get you, you can call it Queenie."

"What if it's a boy?"

"I'll make sure it's a girl," Ava said. "You wouldn't want to call a dog Kingie, would you?"

My wife, who is Japanese, served tea with some dumplings she had made, and I opened a bottle of white wine and brought Ava an ashtray to catch the ashes from her cigarettes.

"You don't smoke?" Ava asked my wife.

"No," Hiromi said. "My brother does. But I never liked it."

"Good for you," Ava said. "I never liked it either, but that didn't stop me from doing it."

"How old were you when you started smoking?" I asked.

"Oh Lord, I grew up playing in tobacco fields," she said. "That's what I was remembering in the hospital, that terrific, lovely smell of tobacco being cured. You had to stay with the tobacco twenty-four hours a day when it was being cured because you had to keep it at a certain temperature. That was in the old days when you had to stoke the fire in these long furnaces. It had to be monitored for six or seven days until the tobacco was cured. I used to love it. I would stay the night with Daddy, sleeping with him."

As Ava puffed and spoke about her early years, my kids came back to look at her. They weren't accustomed to seeing anyone smoke in the house. "Does that burn you?" Hana, our five year-old asked.

"No, honey," Ava said, "but it would burn you if you touched it."

"Does it taste good?"

"Not really. It's just smoke."

"Why do you do it then?"

"Because my Daddy was a tobacco farmer, and these cigarettes are made of tobacco. So I think about him when I smoke."

For a moment I thought Ava was going to offer a puff to my daughters, which would have been a good lesson in understanding why you shouldn't smoke, but she just curled her lips around the cigarette and blew the smoke towards the ceiling. "Kids today are fools to take this up," Ava said, "knowing the dangers of it. But we weren't told. I love cigarettes, I really do. But it's a terrible addiction, worse really than heroin. I always blamed Lana Turner. She had this beautiful gold cigarette case and lighter. I'd never carried cigarettes in my life, just had one when someone offered, or at home I might have a package. But I thought this was the most glamorous thing in the world, this gold case and lighter. So I started carrying them, which was disaster, because once you've got them with you, you're going to use it."

And Ava used it. Two to three packs a day after she got her gold case and lighter. "That's a lot of nicotine. "But I was always nervous, especially when I was working, so it was constant."

She said that she now made it a rule to not carry any cigarettes with her when she went out, unless it was to go shopping. Then she liked to puff. "You can't smoke in the hospital," she said, "and after an hour of exercise, when your lungs are nice, there's no point to come out and start puffing. But I do love cigarettes."

I asked her if she'd like me to admonish her every time she took a cigarette. "That annoys the hell out of me," she said. "I hate lectures. There's this old doctor at St. John's who lectures and I can't stand it. When I want to stop I'll stop. I know the dangers, and I know that my lungs are not as powerful as they used to be. And it's terribly damaging to my double pneumonia."

I turned the subject back to her working in the tobacco fields as a young girl. Her memories were vivid as she described how the leaves were separated, with the bottom leaves being the "trash" that was used for cheap cigars, and the bigger golden leaves near the top of each stalk being more perfect and of higher quality. She spoke about the workers going into the fields on horseback, cutting off the stalks and putting them into a long truck, where it would be unloaded at the barn and tied in batches. "That's where I came in," she said, "handing the tobacco from the truck to the person who tied them. It was very organized." Some of the plants grew to four feet, and the tops had flowers. "Each leaf often had little suckers that had to be taken off and that was a pretty boring job—and messy! My hands would be covered with a thick black gum after just fifteen minutes; it took Octagon soap, which is a powerful soap, to wash that crap off my hands. And that's exactly what goes into my lungs."

She recalled how she would bring fruit jars filled with water to the boys in the field and how on one occasion her brother Melvin promised her a present if she brought them water. "He gave me a big plug of chewing tobacco and I swallowed the damn stuff and got so ill. I'd never been so sick in my life. They thought that was very amusing. I didn't find it amusing at all!"

After the leaves were cured they would become crispy and had to be humidified to make them pliable enough to grade—"first, second, down to trash. Then it was sold in separate piles. But I hear they don't do that any more. Now they just put the whole thing together. But when it was crumbly my nephew Al and I used to take a leaf and crumble it in our hands, then wrap it in a newspaper so it looked like a cigar and we'd puff on those things."

When her mother saw them fiddling around with old newspapers and crappy tobacco, she went to the store and brought back a pack of Philip Morris cigarettes. "Here," she said, "if you're going to do this, don't sneak around and lie to me." That was Ava's first real pack, which she used gingerly. It wasn't until she was a movie star and got her own golden case when her addiction set in.

As we listened to Ava talk and smoke, I found myself inwardly grinning at the fact that Ava Gardner, one of the world's most reclusive and private women, was sitting on a couch in my living room talking about....tobacco! It was fitting, in a way, that she was as down-to-earth as she liked to think she was, but I think Hiromi would have preferred to hear her talk about her love of roses and the smells that came from her mother's kitchen, and I know that while my girls were fascinated watching her smoke, they would have been happier had she actually brought a corgi with her than talk about a dog without a tail that they couldn't really imagine.

"Tell me, Maya, what grade are you in?"

When Maya said she was in second grade, Ava asked her if she had a boyfriend yet, and if she wrote notes to him. Maya nodded, but qualified it with, "We're not married or anything, he's just a friend."

Ava got a kick out of that and Maya went off to play with her friend. "My first beau was when I was in the second grade," Ava said. "I must have been seven or eight. His name was Luther. We used to write love notes to each other when we were just learning to write and I would hide them in this book Momma had. When we were living in the country, Momma was the nurse, and she had this enormous doctor's book which had every disease in it. Whether you had an earache or nosebleed or stubbed toe, it was in that book. And one day Myra found these notes in that book and showed them to Momma. Oh, she was naughty. My heart was broken, and I was so frightened. I thought I would get a whipping for that. But Momma thought it was funny."

"Was he also your first kiss?" I asked.

"Oh no, that came later," Ava said. "I've forgotten his name, but we had been to a New Year's Eve dance and afterwards we were standing on the porch at midnight and he asked if I would kiss him, and he kissed me, just a peck, no serious kissing. But Momma was looking out the window and she came tearing out onto the porch. She yanked me in the house. I was sixteen or seventeen then, and hadn't ever done necking in cars or anything like that. I was brought up very strictly, which was okay, I'm not sorry. I had no great desire to mess around with boys, and it never crossed my mind to go to bed with a boy. But that innocent peck of a kiss, I'd never been so embarrassed in my life. And then she went into a tirade, letting me know that ladies did not do that, they didn't go around kissing boys."

When Ava was ready to return to the Westwood Marquis, Ava gave each of the children a hug. Their playmate, of course, had no idea who Ava was, but at that moment her mother Rose came to pick her up. When Ava stood back up, I made the introduction and Rose's face blanched. "Nice to meet you," Ava said, extending her good hand. "This one yours?"

The look on Rose's face was priceless. "I'm... speechless," she said, and Ava laughed.

"Don't be, honey. I'm just an old gal with a bum arm."

"Oh Ms. Gardner, you're way more than that," Rose gushed. Later Rose would tell her husband how she had held her breath when she was introduced, and would describe Ava as having delicate features, clear skin, sparkling eyes, and an aura of being at peace with herself. She would talk about how they had made eye contact and how that moment in time that lasted perhaps a minute or two affected her in a way she would never forget. "It was," she would say, "like meeting Royalty."

The encounter affected Ava as well. She saw Rose's two other children strapped into car seats in the back of her van as we were getting into my car and she thought about the lives women with children lead. So very different from the life she had lived.

"I never wanted to be a soccer mom," she said as we began driving down the canyon.

"That's the term, isn't it? Mothers who drive all over town taking their kids on play dates, to play sports, to learn music or ballet or gymnastics? But I can see how it could have been rewarding."

"You had examples growing up," I said. "Your own mom, your sisters."

"I talk to my girlfriends and they send me photographs of their families and their grandchildren.....my own sisters, too. I was told I couldn't have children because I had what they called a tipped and infantile uterus. I could have had an operation but I never did. And I never took any precaution, no birth control. But I've never missed not having children. I don't think Bappie has either. Some women feel that terrible sort of emptiness, but I've never had any regrets whatsoever. I wasn't that keen on having babies. With Mickey and Artie I was never pregnant. But with Frank, something must have changed inside me, because I got pregnant. But the time wasn't right so I had it aborted. Wasn't easy, they made me see a shrink first. And I got pregnant again right after, and did away with that one too. Frank didn't know the first time, and found out right after the second. But he knew it wasn't meant to be, not with the lives we were living. I'm very definitely pro-abortion. In those days, it was a tremendous step because it was illegal; you were putting your health and your life in danger. I just never had this great yearning that I've got to have a child." Then her tone changed, from wistful to forceful. "I'm so fed up with those goddamn surrogate mothers. Here is the world, overpopulated—if you must have a child, why not adopt one poor little creature? Rather than it's got to be a piece of yourself—that's a fucking ego trip!"

I never thought of having children as an ego trip myself but I wasn't going to make any defense of natural parenthood with Ava. She had the opportunity and knew how it would have changed her life and career and wasn't willing to make those sacrifices. She was in a volatile relationship with Sinatra, and she was just coming into her own. *Mogambo* in Africa, *The Barefoot Contessa* in Spain and Italy, *Bhowani Junction* in Pakistan, and twenty-one other pictures were still ahead of her. Why settle for the role of mother when you could play goddess?

Nonetheless, seeing my kids, my wife, our home, our life, seemed to have touched Ava in a certain way. "I will get them a corgi," she said as we drove back to her hotel. "They should have a dog."

"I'm sure they'd love one," I said. I told her about the dogs I had as a boy. Fluffy, a white spitz we had when we lived in Brooklyn that we had to give away because we lived in an apartment and people complained. Then there was a brown chow named Teddy that we had when we moved to Long Island, but gave away when my mother was told that such dogs turn on their owners. (My sister said he looked like a teddy bear, thus his name; I thought he looked more like a small lion.) And finally, there was Alex, the fox terrier we rescued from the pound and became my companion until I went to college. Ava had had other dogs before Morgan, and she loved them all, and spoke about them as if they were her children. But it wasn't her dog stories which touched my heart. It was the story of the doll she had when she was my daughter Hana's age.

"I had this doll that I treated like a baby," she said. "I got it for Christmas, which was also my birthday, and I never got presents for both, except cake; I got a chocolate and a coconut cake every birthday. This doll was beautiful, it had golden hair like I did, and its eyes opened and shut. I took it with me everywhere. I talked to it all the time, told it all my secrets. And one day I was playing outside near the schoolhouse when it started to rain. I never minded the rain, it rained all the time, and I loved the way the ground felt under my toes. But this rain became a storm and my father came looking for me and when he found me he brought me back into the house. Momma took off my wet clothes and dried me in front of the fireplace. Then I remembered that I had left my doll outside and I started for the door, but Daddy grabbed me. 'Where're you going, Daughter?' he asked in that voice which said much more than that. 'My doll, Daddy,' I said. 'She's outside in the rain. She's gonna get sick.' 'We'll get it tomorrow,' Daddy said. 'Can't go out in this storm.' But I wanted my doll and I started to cry. 'You heard your father,' Momma said. 'No one's going to take your doll, Ava. You'll catch your death if you go out now.' It was already dark, but I was miserable. I wanted Daddy to get his flashlight and find my doll. I always slept with her. But that night they put me to bed and I was so worried; if I was gonna catch my death going out to find her, what would happen to her being out in that storm all night? Myra told me not to cry, a doll couldn't die because it wasn't alive in the first place. 'You don't know that,' I sobbed. God, I remember this like it was yesterday. I've never talked about this before. But somehow I knew that something dreadful was happening to my doll and the first thing the next morning I ran out to find her and I couldn't. I ran to the trees where I thought I had left her, but the doll had vanished. I looked everywhere, running from tree to tree, looking in the fields, in the barn. I finally found her some distance from the schoolhouse and she was a disaster. Her eyes were stuck together, her face was all peeled, her hair was ratty, and all the life I had seen in her was sucked out of her. I always blamed my Daddy for not letting me save her from that storm. I didn't say anything to him or Momma about it because I knew they felt bad. But something changed in me that day. I can't say what exactly, but it was something important. It was like my best friend had died, and later on, when Daddy died at Newport News when we were living at the Teacherage and we brought him back to North Carolina to be buried, it was the same feeling of loss. Because even though I found that doll, she wasn't the same, she was dead, and I didn't play with her again, just tossed her. Losing that doll was my first great tragedy."

Conversations with Ava Gardner

Early Ava

With Burt Lancaster,
The Killers, 1946

The Naked Maja, 1959

With Clark Gable and
Grace Kelly, *Mogambo*,
1953

Conversations with Ava Gardner

With Frank Sinatra

With Richard Burton, *Night of the Iguana*, 1964

Lawrence Grobel

4

Just a Pretty Little Girl in Hollywood

I ASKED AVA IF she ever had one of those storied aha moments where someone told her she ought to be in pictures. I said that Barbra Streisand once told me about the time she was performing at the Bon Soir nightclub in New York as an unknown, brash teenager, and comedian Larry Storch was headlining, and he said to her, "Kid, you're gonna be a very great star." Jean Harlow, Janet Gaynor, Myrna Loy and Joan Crawford were all supposedly told they "ought to be in pictures." I always felt these stories were somewhat apocryphal, but Ava said it happened to her too. "I'm not surprised about Streisand," she said. "She's a big talent. With me, I was still a kid, 16, in New York with my sister Bappie and her husband, Larry Tarr, who was always trying to promote me. We went to a club that had a live orchestra and Henry Fonda was sitting at a table with some woman. I recognized him from his movies, I think there were a couple with Bette Davis that he made around that time, *Jezebel* and *That*

Certain Woman, and I wondered if he'd give me an autograph. Larry pushed me to go over and ask him so I did. But I was so nervous that I dropped my pen and whatever else I was holding. He was very sweet and signed this piece of paper I had and his date was the one who told me what a lovely girl I was and said, 'You should go to Hollywood.' I bet most Hollywood beauties heard that from someone. Where else would you tell a young, innocent girl who looked like Rita Hayworth or Jean Harlow or Marilyn to go?"

From asking for Fonda's autograph to signing ones of her own took just three years for young Ava. But the autographs she signed at nineteen had a "Mrs." in front of her first name and a "Rooney" after it. How she got from virgin Ava to the first wife of the multitalented, egotistical, high profile, 21 year-old Mickey Rooney was very much a True Hollywood Story.

It started with a photograph that Larry Tarr took of her when she was 16. Tarr recognized Ava's beauty and captured it in a portrait. He put a bonnet on her head, tied it with a bow underneath her soon-to-be-famous cleft chin, and had her gaze dreamily off camera, her eyebrows perfectly accentuating her eyes, and her perfect nose and sensuous lips filling her unblemished milk white face. She was wearing a short sleeved patterned summer dress, her bare arms showing from just above her elbow to just below the shoulder. It was a portrait of a very beautiful girl who may not have been as innocent as she seemed—though in fact she was still quite innocent. Tarr put this picture in the window of his photographic studio on the corner of Fifth Avenue and 63rd Street and a man named Barney Duhan saw it. Duhan worked as an errand boy in the law department of Loews, Inc., and thought he might get a date with Ava if he presented himself as a scout for MGM, which was a part of Loews. He never got the date, but Tarr was quick enough to send MGM a slew of additional photos of Ava, and in that proverbial one-in-a-million chance, Marvin Schenck in the MGM talent department asked her to come in for an audition.

"You've probably heard that old story: 'She can't act. She can't talk. She can't walk. She's great,'" Ava said. "I read that shit about me a million times. What actually happened was that I did a test in New York in some cat's office. They gave me a scene to read and I couldn't act. Let's face it, I was the first to be eliminated in high school plays. I had no training whatsoever, and this big Southern accent, sort of a mix between Virginia and North Carolina. Once they realized I simply couldn't do a scene, they did an interview test, which was purely photographic. It was for people who were beautiful and had no talent. And that was me: there wasn't a thing that I could do. I was just a pretty little girl. They had me walk across the room, pick up a vase of flowers and bring them to the camera, look, smile, and they just photographed every angle, right, left, up and down. And then they asked, 'What is your name? Where are you from?' Being completely innocent about the whole thing, I wasn't terribly nervous. Acting wasn't a lifelong ambition. I was going to be a secretary."

She wasn't kidding. After graduating high school at seventeen, she spent a year taking secretarial courses at Atlantic Christian College, in Winston, North Carolina, learning shorthand and typing. "I didn't belong to any sororities or clubs, and lived at home. They had a contest for the Most Beautiful Girl in the school. After the votes were counted, I came in second to a girl named Fitzgerald. She wasn't that pretty, but she was very wealthy, she lived on campus, and belonged to a sorority. They put her picture up as a full page in the paper, and I got a little picture. My picture was really beautiful. But there was a kid who helped count the votes and he told me that I had gotten more votes than she did.

"I wasn't really upset. What did it matter if you won a beauty contest at a Christian college? I had other interests. I was very good at sports. They had a basketball team, which I wasn't on, but one night I went to a game wearing a little red skirt and sweater. Some of the players fouled out and they didn't have enough to finish the game, so I was spotted in the bleachers and they asked me to be a substitute. I was the only one on the court not wearing a uniform. I was excited to be asked and as soon as I got my hands on the ball I went flying to the basket, thinking, 'Jesus, nobody's guarding me; this is fantastic!' I made a beautiful layup and heard people screaming and laughing. I scored for the other team. I really was humiliated that night. They took me out of the game after that. I don't think I had ever been so embarrassed. Good God, how they laughed."

It wasn't the first time people laughed at Ava. When the family moved from North Carolina to Virginia, Ava was enrolled into a seventh grade class. Her country accent "wasn't very chic," she recalled. "The teacher asked me all these personal questions in front of the class. 'What is your name? Where are you from? What does your father do?' By the time I got around to saying my Daddy's a farmer, the other children were all laughing at me. What was so fucking funny about that, I ask you? But they were roaring and over time my accent changed to a Virginia accent, which was much citified. And then when we went back to North Carolina, oh brother, I heard it from people there, saying 'She's putting on airs.' So, you can't win."

In 1941 MGM gave her a seven-year contract for $35 a week. She moved to Hollywood, and her accent was one of the things she worked on. "I thought I was making fifty dollars a week," Ava said, the bitter taste still in her mouth, "but it turned out to be $35 because twelve weeks of the year you were on layoff. It was white slavery, and it lasted for seventeen years." But when Ava was signed, no one saw any great acting potential. She was just one of the "cheesecake girls," who had a great figure, beautiful smile, and legs that looked good in a swimsuit or swinging from a broomstick wearing a witch's hat and holding a Halloween pumpkin.

"There were quite a few of us," Ava recalled. "They called it a stable of young starlets, but there were young men as well. All were just beautiful, with no talent, and no job. My first two years I did gobs of publicity. I'd go to this photo studio when they needed one of us to advertise a film or take a photo for a newspaper. They'd ask, 'Who has a good pair of legs?' 'Who has good breasts and isn't working?' And it was always Ava, because I was never working. So I would pose with skis on sand dunes at the beach. One of the funniest ones was on a particularly hot day in Los Angeles, where it soared into the hundreds. They brought out this enormous hundred-pound block of ice. I put on a red and white candy-stripe bathing suit and they put an electric fan on the ice and a paper fan in my hand and I posed sitting on that ice. That's the kind of crap I did, and there must be ten million photographs of me doing shit like that. It was tedious, but it was better than just sitting on your bum."

"What about acting lessons?" I asked. "Surely, you studied with an acting coach when you first arrived. You were, after all, pretty green."

"We would make appointments to meet with the drama coach, Lillian Burns, but when we'd get there, some star like Lana Turner or Margaret O'Brien would turn up and we'd wind up sitting in her office, wasting the day waiting. Burnsie was something else. She wore lots of jewelry and had a mirror in her office. Even if you got in there for a lesson, she'd give you a scene and she'd play all the parts in front of the mirror.

She was rather ugly, a short little Jewish woman with bangs. And she'd do all the acting in that mirror, posing with her rings. That was our drama coach.

"But when we couldn't get time with her, we'd go over to Gertrude Vogeler's office, way out on the back lot. She was a sweet old woman with white hair and a million cats. I loved her. Accents were worked on and if you happened to have one line in a film, she would work on it with you. I spoke a lot with my throat and she put me through all the vowels and all the sounds. It was purely from the throat and she'd try to get it down in the chest and then from the stomach. She was a round, little woman and I'd sit across from her at this small desk and she would bounce up and down and say, 'Sit on it, my beauty, sit on it.' You had to sit on your voice."

Ava was living with her sister Bappie, who had to quit her job working at I. Miller's in New York to chaperone her younger sister in Hollywood. Bappie landed a job at I. Magnin's in downtown L.A. selling handbags, which gave them enough to pay for a small apartment. When Ava got back from the studio she was supposed to practice what she had learned from her voice and drama coaches. "Unfortunately, darling, I didn't do much about learning my craft," she freely admitted. "I really didn't. I was lazy. I think I would have been a hell of a lot better actress had I worked and taken it more seriously. I never had the proper respect for acting, which is foolish. Quite often, I learned my lines on the way to the studio. I was always on time, and I knew the lines. I just thought, if I had nothing else to contribute, at least I could do that, and then just rely on the director, which is what I always did. But recently I've seen two films of mine and I thought, damn, I've underestimated myself. I wasn't *that* bad."

I agreed. While films like *Pandora and the Flying Dutchman* or *The Little Hut* seemed a bit slight, with Ava delivering most of her lines without much passion, she was fun to watch in any number of her sixty-odd films, especially *The Killers, Mogambo, One Touch of Venus, The Barefoot Contessa, On the Beach, Seven Days in May*, and *The Night of the Iguana*. I wondered if she had learned anything at all when she studied, however briefly, with Lillian Burns.

"Not a fucking thing," Ava said. "Half the time, as I told you, we didn't get our lesson because somebody else would butt in. And when we did get in with her, we would take our scene, either from Shakespeare or from modern plays, and work on that. But she did all the acting. We were just young starlets– Donna Reed, Esther Williams. Esther actually came in with a splash, literally, because she had this great swimming talent, and she was very beautiful. They built things around her and for her, including a special stage with a pool. Her spectacles made a lot of money. But she was just as lousy an actress as I was."

The refreshing thing about Ava was that she never had any pretensions. She succeeded far beyond anything she had imagined when she was growing up, and she had no illusions about comparing herself with some of the great actresses of her era, like Bette Davis, Ingrid Bergman, Joanne Woodward, or Barbara Stanwyck. "I really had very little to contribute," she said. "So when I started out, I often was a hat check girl or an extra, or played in mob scenes or dancing scenes, just to have the experience of being on a set. And many times I didn't even have a line. I spent years at that."

One would imagine that once she saw the limelight, even from the sidelines, she had to understand the allure and the perks of stardom. I asked if being beautiful was enough.

"I didn't want to be mediocre," she said, "but I had no terrible, great ambition to be a big star. It sort of just gradually happened without my doing very much about it. Had I worked at it I may not have been a bigger star, but I would have been a better actress. Maybe I was better the way I was. But I don't know why I was a star. You know what they once told me? That when my films would run, with each clip that you saw there was another clip that went through the camera that you didn't see, and that subliminal clip was a photograph of me over the years. It was supposed to reach your subconscious, without you realizing it. I read that they did this with advertising, to get you to buy Coke or whatever while you were watching a movie, but I often wondered if that was the reason that people cottoned to me."

One major star definitely cottoned to her, and though she spurned his advances in the beginning, Mickey Rooney told himself and everyone else that she was the girl he was going to marry. "The more successful I was," Rooney wrote in his 1965 autobiography, "the more successful I had to become. I'd acted, sung, danced, drunk, gambled. I'd met President Roosevelt and Henry Ford. My face was postered all over America. What was there left for me at twenty? Try marriage. That was where this drive pushed me next. My drive and the beauty of Ava Gardner."

Rooney wasn't exaggerating when he spoke of his face being plastered all over America. From ages six through fourteen he appeared as Mickey McGuire in over fifty silent "short" comedies, and by the time he met Ava he had been featured or had starred in over forty full length movies, including *A Midsummer's Night Dream, Captains Courageous, Boys Town,* and the title characters in *The Adventures of Huckleberry Finn* and *Young Tom Edison*. He was the first teenager to be nominated for a Best Actor Oscar for *Babes in Arms* and was most popular for the eight Andy Hardy musicals he did opposite Judy Garland before his 21st birthday.

"He was the most talented man I've ever known," Ava said, adding, "I talked to him the other day—he came to the hospital– and I heard the Jesus Christ routine. He's a reborn Christian. A Jesus man. He kept on about being made in the image of God, and that I was all right, there was nothing wrong with me. What a load of crap! But in those days he wasn't into the Jesus routine. He was into sports, working, and pretty girls. I met him on the set when they were showing me around the studio. He was doing *Babes on Broadway* with Judy Garland. It made an impression because I was such a young girl. It was fascinating to watch the two of them together."

Rooney never forgot the first time he laid eyes on Ava, because of the way she looked—"like a princess"—and the way he looked, dressed in woman's clothes with a fruit bowl on his head as he impersonated Carmen Miranda.

"I don't know how he got in touch with me afterwards," Ava said, "but he did. He found me, and asked if I would go out with him. I pretended that I had a date. I had only been in Hollywood a few days and didn't know a soul, but there was that old Southern thing, you know, 'I'm busy.'"

Rooney didn't understand how an "extra" could rebuff his advances. His ego was as large as the Hollywood Bowl and his reputation as a ladies man, even though he was a *short* ladies man, was well known and a cause of concern to MGM, who preferred a more wholesome image for their young star.

"Ava didn't give a damn who I was, or what I was, or what I could do for her, or how much money I was making," Rooney remembered. "She seemed to be disinterested in the box office king of the world."

Not so, according to Ava. "I was attracted to him and couldn't wait until he called again to ask me out, which he did very quickly. We went to the Luau, where I had my first rum drink, which was divine. We both loved to dance so we went to the Coconut Grove a lot and that's where he started sneaking me drinks in coffee cups, because I was still underage. Christ, I wish I hadn't started. Some of the things that I regret most in my life happened when I was drinking. I'm just not good with alcohol. I'm not in control. And I don't give a damn what time of the day it is or when it is, I just drink too much. It's very unfortunate. "

Metro threw an enormous party for Rooney when he turned twenty-one and Ava got to meet Louis B. Mayer for the first time, though she was more impressed seeing "all the glamour queens," among them Lana Turner and Judy Garland. Rooney, though, had fallen for Ava and was determined to make her his own.

"I invaded every aspect of her life," he wrote. "I was always available for such services as chauffeuring, dinner purchasing, squiring, impersonating, and proposing. Ava in turn was unavailable. She gave me neither her heart, nor her body."

When I read some of Rooney's quotes to her, Ava would laugh or smile as she exhaled smoke and remembered how she was then, and how quickly things changed.

"Oh God, that's not funny, but he's terribly sweet. And accurate. But it was sort of a game that Southern girls played, to be unattainable. I still believe it. I'm very old-fashioned. I disapprove of all this living together and having bastard babies. Why don't they get married, if they care that much about each other?"

For a gal who had tried and failed at it three times, I was surprised to hear her say this. But Ava was a romantic. She was also a realist. Marriage, she realized after Mr. Sinatra, was not her thing. Playing the field, having fun, keeping one's distance is how she learned to live her life.

"It was an Andy Hardy kind of courtship," Mickey Rooney said about that time of innocence for both of them. Neither had yet experienced what it was like to be married. He was still living in Encino with his mother and his stepfather, an accountant at MGM and "not a very nice man," according to Ava. "Mickey's father was married to a very sweet lady, and I got along fine with her. In fact, I always said, if I got along as well with my husbands as I did with their mothers, my marriages would have been more successful."

"She gave me her lips for a goodnight kiss," Rooney wrote of their early dates. "She gave me soft hands to hold. She gave me nothing more."

Ava thought that Rooney was "very much a gentleman. There was the odd kiss or two and a little necking. Bappie was always around. She and Mickey were great chums. But she was so careful that we didn't go to bed together. One night we asked Bappie if it was all right if we slept together for an hour or two. We were living at the Hollywood Wilcox then. It was a dreadful damn place, one bedroom. It was innocent—I remembered that my sister Myra had asked Bappie if she could do that with the guy she was going to marry before he went into the Navy, and they did. I'd never had any experience whatsoever before, and when

Bappie said OK, Mickey didn't force himself on me, which I admired. And he was great fun."

The fun turned serious rather quickly, as Mickey mistakenly thought he was ready to settle down. Ava wasn't really thinking about it.

"I didn't know he was going to propose, but I was delighted when he asked. With me, it's always immediate or nothing. I fall in love quickly or not at all. I've never sort of grown to love. I was very much in love with him. But I was still eighteen when he proposed and I told him we had to wait until I turned nineteen, because Momma was nineteen when she married."

They also had to wait for L.B. Mayer's blessing, which wasn't immediately forthcoming. Rooney might have looked upon the Metro boss as a father figure, but Mayer saw Rooney more in box-office returns. At the time, Mickey Rooney was their Golden Goose. He had a certain image, and that was as Andy Hardy—fresh, jubilant, happy-go-lucky, a pal of Judy's, still a kid. Ava, even at nineteen, was a bombshell and her talent, if she had any, had yet to be discovered. She was probably, Mayer thought, a gold digger, hitching her future to his star. He didn't want to give his blessing. What he hadn't counted on was Rooney telling him that he was going to marry Ava no matter what, and he was sure he could find another studio who would appreciate his talents.

"We had to ask L.B. Mayer for permission to get married," Ava said. "I'll never forget that day. We went up to his office, and I'd never been there before. I waited in the outer office with his elderly secretary while Mickey went in to see Uncle L.B., and she said to me, 'Just remember one thing, young lady. You can't change the spots on a leopard.' What a dreadful thing to say. But, of course, she was right."

Mayer wasn't pleased that his young superstar was going to put himself out of the fantasies of so many of his female fans, but he relented, on the condition that their wedding be small and out of the way, so fans and reporters wouldn't be there. "It was a soreheaded demand," Ava said. "But we let Metro arrange it in Ballard, a place that wasn't even a town, located in the foothills of the Santa Ynez Mountains. It looked like country to me. We went there early in the morning; took two hours to drive. Seven people—Bappie, the publicist, Mickey's mother, father and stepfather, me and Mickey. Metro wanted to keep it from becoming a circus, since Mickey was number one at the box office at that time. He was a very important property to them. That's the way they thought of people—as property, for God's sake. Not as human beings. So it could have been a madhouse. But it was done very quietly and with dignity. No press at all. I wore a tailored blue suit. I couldn't afford a big wedding dress and I wouldn't accept Mickey buying me one. I didn't accept charity—that's just how I was brought up. Mickey is about 5'4" and I'm two inches taller, so I learned to slouch. I took my heels off for the photographs and I had a good way of making myself look shorter. It didn't matter because he came on bigger than life; he made himself tall. It was a religious ceremony in front of a preacher, love and obey, very old fashioned. I was very nervous and frightened. God, I don't know which is worse, getting married or getting divorced. Both are awful. And you know what? I cried. I always cry at weddings, including my own. And I don't cry at funerals. Isn't that funny?"

What Ava remembered about the wedding party was that "Everybody got drunk and there was quite a brawl later on in the day." Ava wasn't clear about who was brawling, but it wasn't the newlyweds, who, along with MGM publicist Les Petersen, soon took off up the coast to Monterey, where they had reserved two rooms at the Del Monte Hotel near Carmel. It was time to deflower the virgin princess.

"I was a virgin when we married, it's true. I told Bappie I needed to get some new panties, because I always slept in panties, and she said, 'You are not going to sleep in panties the first night.' So we went out and bought some pretty nighties. And that first night at the Del Monte Hotel was a fiasco. Les Petersen had brought a bottle of champagne to the room and I didn't really drink in those days. I kept hanging on to Les because I was scared to death. He would say 'Good night,' and I would say, 'Let's have another glass of champagne.' So we had four glasses and finally Les left and I was on my own. I was naked underneath my nightie–one frightened, shy young lady, I'll tell you that. But it turned out well. I caught on very, very quickly."

"Do you actually remember it, since you had four glasses of champagne?" I wondered.

"Of course I remember it! Jesus Christ, what woman doesn't remember her first night in bed with a man?"

The cigarettes were mounting as we talked, and Ava blamed me for it. "You are good for at least a pack," she said. "You have no idea how difficult this is, to know that little bugger is down there." She was referring to my tape recorder. I was trying to get more intimate details of her wedding night, but she wasn't in the mood to be any more explicit. So we talked about their honeymoon, where Ava learned about her husband's passion....for golf. He went out every morning to play Pebble Beach, leaving Ava behind to wonder what her role as wife was supposed to be. After a few days there they headed to San Francisco and checked into the Palace Hotel. MGM had arranged for Mickey to do some publicity for his film *Life Begins for Andy Hardy* and then they took the Super Chief train east, stopping in Chicago, Boston, New York, North Carolina, and Washington D.C., as Mickey entertained the troops and Ava was the eye candy.

"We were invited to the White House because Mickey had done a lot of things for the March of Dimes," Ava said. "President Roosevelt congratulated us and shook our hands. He was very sweet and warm, and Eleanor was divine, a brilliant woman with a great personality who really made an impact when you met her. She showed us all around the White House. It was very informal. 'And this is Franklin's rooooooom.' We were invited to one of the president's Fireside Chats while he was broadcasting. That was marvelous. He was a great speaker; he didn't use any notes or cards, he just sat in his wheelchair with folded arms talking into the microphone. It was all extemporaneous and from his heart. And it was mesmerizing."

When they returned to Los Angeles, they moved into a two bedroom apartment in the Wilshire Palms near Westwood, owned by Red Skelton. Ava thought they would settle into some sort of married life routine, where she would cook and Mickey would be home each night for dinner. But that wasn't the way it turned out. Rooney liked to party and went out with his buddies nearly every night, and brought his wife when she felt like it. In the mornings, he would get up earlier than needed, so he could drive Ava to the studio, where she was still struggling to get noticed. He soon tired of losing that hour every morning, preferring to play golf if he wasn't required at the studio, and gave her the car—a red Lincoln Continental convertible—as a gift. Ava learned to drive. She also learned that her husband was an addictive gambler.

"Whatever he was involved in—golf, work, horses—they had to put a direct line in for him so he could call his bookies on the set. He would give me wonderful presents whenever he won big and the next week whatever he gave me went back because of his losses betting on the horses. The first thing he ever gave me was a beautiful topaz ring. We were at Ciro's with another couple. He opened this box at the table. I was embarrassed. Mickey loved to give presents, even though most of them went back. It became like a game, which wasn't a problem for me, because I'd have the jewelry for a week before giving it up, but I always knew there'd be another big win and I'd get another present."

But their marriage wasn't destined to last. Mickey was too young, too wild, and too full of himself to understand how to be a husband to a woman like Ava. And Ava had no real knowledge of men, especially one who was used to adulation and fawning. Within months of their marriage they became sparring partners. Once she threw an inkwell at his head. She cut up furniture with a knife. She threatened to kill him if she ever got pregnant. She kicked him out of their house after eight months and they filed for divorce soon after. He cried when he realized it was over between them.

"I thought that marriage was a small dictatorship in which the husband is the dictator and the wife is the underling," Rooney later wrote. "What an impossible son of a bitch I must have been. To this day, I don't think Ava has forgiven me for my selfishness, my stupidity and my clumsiness."

5

The Billionaire & the Clarinet Player

"AFTER MICKEY AND I SEPARATED, I got a call from a friend saying there was a man who wanted to meet me, and his name was Howard Hughes. I thought she said Howard Hawks, the director, who wanted to see me for a film. Kay came by with Johnny Meyers, who worked for Hughes as sort of a pimp, but not really. He entertained Howard's girlfriends when Howard was busy or just didn't feel like going to nightclubs. After Johnny checked me out he asked if I would be willing to meet his boss. I was still thinking it was Howard Hawks. "Sure," I said. He took me to one of Howard's many houses and during the course of the evening I realized this man wasn't who I thought he was; he was Howard Hughes."

Howard Hughes, in 1943, was one of the world's most intriguing and diversified figures in America. He inherited his wealth from his father, who had invented a way to drill for petroleum in inaccessible places. When he was eleven he built a radio transmitter; at twelve, a motorized bicycle. His great interest was in aviation. In 1932 he founded Hughes Aircraft and in 1939 took over TWA. He loved to fly, and set two airspeed records before setting a third by flying around the world in 91 hours. In 1939 he was awarded a Congressional Gold Medal for advancing the science of aviation. His second passion was the movies and he produced a number of films beginning in 1927, including *The Front Page, Hell's Angels* and *Scarface*. For *The Outlaw* he designed a special bra for leading lady Jane Russell. His third great passion was Women.

"I didn't know anything about him," Ava said. "I didn't know about his reputation or his great wealth or his thing about airplanes and jetting around the world. I just knew that as soon as I got divorced from Mickey, Howard entered my life and I couldn't get rid of him for the next fifteen years, no matter who I was with or who I married. He was Johnny-on-the-Spot, appearing after every one of my marriages or every broken love affair—and sometimes he had arranged to have them broken. He kept on and on and on, wanting to marry me, promising me anything in the world. But I never loved him. It just never clicked. He could be charming, sweet, and kind to me, but he could also be cruel to other people.

"I got to know him very well. We were both Capricorns, about fifteen years apart. He was a Christmas Eve child, too. He was extremely shy to the point of a sickness and that caused all that reclusive routine. We were very similar about that. He simply didn't want a lot of other people around. He was frightened to go out. It wasn't that he didn't want to be seen—he was terrified. But he loved to dance and he loved music. We would go to places after hours and Howard would take the place over and keep the orchestra. He was not much of a drinker—he drank tall rum drinks—and he didn't smoke. But he loved to dance. We went to San Francisco one time and had a good time until the shit hit the fan. The shit was *always* hitting the fan!"

Hughes was also an extremely jealous man and Ava experienced his jealousy in such a cruel way that she was, at first, afraid to even discuss it, almost as if, so many years later, the ghost of Howard Hughes (he died in 1976) might come to silence her. But the story was too ripe not to tell.

"This happened when I had moved with Bappie to my house in Nichols Canyon. It was during the war and Howard had gone to Washington because he had some high secret information to pass on. He had been to the White House, meeting with all the top brass. When he returned, he flew into Burbank airport and Johnny Meyers picked him up. I was supposed to go with Johnny but I didn't because I had a date with Mickey. Even though we were divorced, I still saw him on occasion. Howard asked Johnny where I was and he just said that I couldn't make it. He told Johnny to drive to my house, convinced he would find me in bed with another guy. Bappie was there, and Charlie Guest, who worked for Hughes and was dating my sister. I was asleep upstairs when Howard entered my room. I was livid, absolutely furious at this intrusion, and started screaming, 'How dare you?' He backed away and said, 'We'll discuss this downstairs.' I put a robe on and went down. Howard was angry that I hadn't gone to the airport. I told him I hadn't wanted to go. He asked where I had been. I said, 'None of your business. But if you want to know, I went out with Mickey.' That put him in a rage like I had never seen before. Howard was a gentle man, but he lost control completely. All of a sudden, BOOM! I was knocked across my face and fell into this chair. He jumped at me and started to pound on my face until it was a mess. This was the first time anybody had ever hit me. When he finally stopped and went to leave, I looked for some weapon to attack him. There was a bronze bell on the bar with a very long handle. I picked it up and walked towards the living room as he was going out and yelled at him. 'Howard!' I screamed, because he was very deaf and I knew he couldn't hear. As he turned I let go with this bell and conked him in the temple, splitting his face open and knocking out two teeth. He went down and I was still in such a rage that I picked up this mahogany chair and went at him again. He was scared, cowering in the corner as I lifted the chair over my head. I was going to kill him. It was my maid who saved his life. She walked in just as I was about to bring down that chair on

Howard's head, and she started clapping her hands and calling me by my first name, 'Ava! Ava! Ava!' She had always called me Miss Gardner, so it startled me. I looked at her and she shouted, 'Stop it!' and I put down the chair. If she hadn't come in, I'm sure I would have continued. Thank God I didn't because I'd probably still be in jail."

"Where was your sister and his assistant during all this?"

"They appeared right after, darling. Here I was, wandering around with my face all black and blue, but they didn't pay any attention to me. They were on the phone getting doctors for Howard. They must have lined up five doctors—a plastic surgeon, a brain surgeon, his own personal doctor. The maid brought me a piece of raw steak to put on my face, which was a mess. And Howard had this dentist who, he swore to me later, put his teeth back under the gum and they grew back together. Howard said if bones can grow back together, why shouldn't teeth? So I guess he had the first implants long before anyone knew it was possible."

I couldn't help but reference what she had told me two years earlier about how George C. Scott had pummeled her face. With Scott, it was alcohol that did him in. But with Hughes, it was just jealousy. Again, there was something about Ava that drove men to behave like beasts.

"All I can tell you is that I don't enjoy being beaten. I'm not one of those people who sit around and get beaten up," Ava said. "I felt sorry for George, maybe because his ex-wife had written to me, begging me to not press charges against him. So did all sorts of his friends. But with Howard, I had no sympathy for what he did to me. It was years before I saw him again, and that was after Artie."

Husband Number Two, Artie Shaw, came into her life when her friend Frances Heflin thought she'd find him attractive. She was right. He was handsome; he was a Big Band leader; he played a mean clarinet; and he was a man of taste and independence and, according to some, a genius. He was certainly a man worth dating, which Ava did for eight months before agreeing to move in to his English Tudor house on Bedford Drive in Beverly Hills. He had already been married twice, but Ava had fallen in love and agreed to be Number Three.

"When I first met him," she told me, "he said, 'You are the healthiest woman I've ever met, mentally, physically and emotionally.'" He called her a "goddess" and told a reporter, "I would stare at her, literally stare, in wonder."

"We hadn't been married five minutes," Ava said, "when he decided I should go to an analyst, so I started psychoanalysis. Artie was a pseudo-intellectual. He had a great oral diarrhea, always spouting off, you know? He really was a very bright man, extremely well read, but he made such a display of it. I was constantly being put down because I didn't know everything. I had very little formal education. It got to a point where I was beginning to doubt my own intelligence and took an I.Q. test. Turned out to be very high. The doctor said, 'You have nothing to worry about. You may not know very much because you haven't used your brain a great deal, but you've got the power to know and to learn.' That made me feel a hell of a lot better, especially when Artie had his friends visit.

"Artie didn't like many people, including Bappie, who didn't like him much either. Artie didn't even like his own mother! So during the time I was married to Artie I didn't see Bappie a great deal. She never came over and stayed with us. But sometimes we'd entertain, like when Peter Viertel and his wife Virginia Ray would come over. That's when I met Peter. He and Artie were in the Navy somewhere in the South Pacific together. Virginia had been married to Budd Schulberg when she was very young. I was very jealous of her when she told me that Schulberg had sent her to the university and she'd become a very well-educated young lady. One day Virginia and I went to lunch at the Farmer's Market. She was pregnant then and we got to talking and she blurted out that she was jealous of me because I had this beautiful body, and I was always swimming while she was just waddling around. I told her, 'I was petrified of you because you were so bright and you could talk to my husband and I couldn't. I felt so inferior.' After that we became good friends."

"What happened to her?" I asked.

"She came to a very sad end. She burned to death. She and Peter were separated. She was ill and was smoking in the bathroom. She had locked the door and they couldn't get to her in time. It was very tragic."

"How often did your feeling of inferiority lead to fights between you and Shaw?" I asked.

"Often," Ava said. "Whenever we'd have a fight, I'd run away. Usually I'd go swimming in someone else's pool. I'd come home with my hair dripping wet and he'd ask, 'Where the hell have you been?' I'd shake my head like a shaggy dog and smile. I did this with all my husbands—I'd run away, but I always came home. I just liked to worry them. But I didn't win many arguments with Artie. He made the rules and I went along with them. I was madly in love with him, but I wasn't treated as an equal, as a wife; I was treated as sort of his little pet."

"It's hard to stay madly in love with anyone," I said. "Especially someone who doesn't treat you the way you would like."

"Well, to tell you the truth," Ava said, "it didn't wear off. It never did. With all three of my marriages, I left, but I was still in love with all three of them. Gradually, it wore off, but oh God, it broke my heart. I was absolutely mad about Artie. We just simply couldn't get along. There were no beatings or any sort of mistreatment, we just had terrible fights.

"One time after one of our fights I left home, got in my car, and started driving as fast as I could. We'd been drinking bourbon old-fashioneds and I was feeling no pain. I headed for Van and Frances Heflin's house on Veteran Avenue, just a few miles away. I was really flying when a cop came up behind me, siren going, red light flashing. That startled me, so I put my foot down on the gas pedal and went faster, faster, faster. When I got to Van Heflin's house I stopped. There were two cops and one had his pistol drawn which he stuck right in my face. I started screaming at him like a goddamn fool. He could have shot me. He certainly didn't recognize me because I hadn't done any major movie yet to warrant that. I opened the car door, yelling all the time, and just started running to Van's house. Van was at the door because of the commotion and as soon as I saw him I said, 'Jesus Van, I've been drinking. Can you smell it?' And he said, 'Yeah, you sure can.' 'What am I gonna do?' I said. The cops were standing by my car watching this. 'The best thing to do is to go out there and try to make friends with them,' he said. So I did. They had me walk a line, which I did very well. No matter how drunk I got, I was always able to walk a straight line. And I got away with it. I shouldn't have, but I did."

"And did you tell Artie about it when you went home? Or was the love between you beginning to diminish by then?"

"It was never a gradual wearing out of love. I had gotten to the point where I couldn't eat because of all our fights. I went to a doctor and he said the only thing he could think of at that time was to give myself injections of insulin. It was supposed to give me a false appetite. I learned to do that, which was pretty horrible because I can't hack needles. And then, Christ, we'd start an argument and I couldn't eat, and then I would practically go into shock so I would have to eat sugar very quickly. I was in a terrible state. I was very thin. Artie had sold his house on Bedford Drive and we had moved to some little place he rented in the Valley. I knew I had to find my own place and it was hard to find places because it was during the war. I wandered around Beverly Hills looking for a place to live and ran into Minna Wallis, producer Hal Wallis's sister. She saw how I looked and said, 'God, what is wrong with you, child?' When I told her I was looking for a place, she invited me to live with her. So I stayed with her for a while until I found a place of my own. I was in a bad state. I was still crazy about Artie and when he called me one day, I was thrilled. I went flying over to his office like a damn fool to see him. He wanted to see me too—to ask me if I minded if he went to Mexico to get a quick divorce so he could marry Kathleen Winsor. I was crushed. I said, 'Yes, of course.' So that's what he did, he married her. Lasted a year or two I think. And that was my marriage to Artie Shaw."

There was obviously a great deal more to explore about her time with Shaw. Her lack-of-education complex led her to enroll in English literature and economics extension courses at UCLA. She had learned to play chess from a chess master and the one time Shaw agreed to play with her, she beat him. The analysis she began then was something she continued throughout her life, so she had done a great deal of reflection and self-exploration. The marriage had only lasted a year when it ended in October 1946. Ava was just 24 and had already married and divorced two of the most creative and talented men in the film and music businesses. There'd be some hard times ahead, and a few movies where she'd become a star herself before she fell for Frank Sinatra, a combination of Rooney and Shaw, and a talent unlike any other. During the lows and the highs she was never alone because she had found a new best friend and confidante in a black maid named Mearene Jordan.

"I was pretty down after Artie. The only good thing that happened to me right after that marriage dissolved was finding Reenie, this wonderful black girl who started working for me. Her sister Tracy Jordon had been working for some friends of Artie. I wasn't making much money from Metro and I found a tiny apartment on Olympic Blvd. I really needed a maid and Tracy told me her sister was coming out from St. Louis and didn't have a job. I said I couldn't pay her very much and she said it didn't matter, she just needed a home and food. So Reenie started to work for me. We were the same age and we struggled together. Things were tough. Part of my contract was doing commercials, which I had to do regularly. I didn't get a fucking penny extra for any of them—I hate to think how much money I could make today. When I did a Lux toilet soap commercial, which I hated, they would send me a box of soap at the end of the month. Reenie would take it to the grocery store and trade it for Ivory. That's how poor we were. Reenie went through the really lean years. She traveled with me and knows more about me than any human being alive—more than my sister, more than any friends. She went through all my love affairs, my brief but passionate times with Howard Duff and Robert Taylor, my unsuccessful attempts to seduce Bob Mitchum, the craziness with Howard Hughes, and my marriage and divorce with Frank. She knows it all."

Ava fell in love with Frank Sinatra in Palm Springs in 1949. He had been at the top of the music charts but had fallen on hard times while Ava's star was rising dramatically after *The Killers* in 1946, followed by *The Hucksters* (with her youthful idol Clark Gable), and *Singapore* (with Fred MacMurray) in1947, *One Touch of Venus* in 1948, and *The Bribe* (with Robert Taylor), *The Great Sinner* (with Gregory Peck), and *East Side, West Side* (with Barbara Stanwyck, James Mason and Van Heflin) in 1949. By Valentine's Day, 1950, Nancy Sinatra, Frank's wife and mother of his three children, publicly announced their separation and Ava was cast as the home wrecker. Catholic priests denounced her from their pulpits and the Legion of Decency called for a ban of her movies. Ava couldn't understand any of this. She had fallen madly in love with a man. He madly loved her back. So what if he was unhappily married and his name was Frank Sinatra?

6

Ol' Blue Eyes & the Gift Giver

IT WOULD TAKE ANOTHER TEMPESTUOUS year before Nancy Sinatra finally signed the divorce papers. Frank and Ava's love affair was followed by paparazzi around the world, as the two volatile lovers had no qualms about openly expressing their emotions in restaurants, nightclubs, hotel rooms, sporting events, or parking lots.

Frank often threatened to kill himself. Once he fired a gun into a hotel mattress with Ava listening on the phone in another room, convinced he had taken his life. Another time in Tahoe after they had a huge fight, Ava drove back to Los Angeles only to get a call that Frank was suicidal. She drove back to Tahoe to find him in bed wondering where she had gone. Theirs was a combustible relationship—two stubborn, headstrong stars used to getting their way, constantly clashing over matters of trust and loyalty. While they both loved each other more than they had loved anyone else, their love was fueled by drunken doubts of each other's faithfulness. Sinatra would ask her if she'd rather be with Howard Hughes or Artie Shaw or one of her bullfighters; Ava would tell him to shut up and then bring up all the women Sinatra romanced. Lamps would get thrown, hotel rooms got wrecked. One time, even a boat was sunk. Ava would run away, Sinatra would pout. It was a match made more in hell than in heaven. The stars were not aligned when these two wildly independent larger-than-life characters came together.

But when Sinatra needed her, she was there for him. And when a part came up that might change his life, he turned to Ava for help.

"Frank had read the script for *From Here to Eternity* and he fell in love with the part of Angelo Maggio and desperately wanted to do it," Ava said. "The poor guy was literally without a job. He said all he could do was play saloons and crappy night clubs. His contract with Metro was finished—in fact, they had terminated it. His contract with Columbia Records was also terminated. He was in a terrible state. His ego and self-esteem was at its lowest ever. And mine was practically at its peak. So it was hell for him and a terrible thing to go through because I had to work. He was such a proud man, such a giving man—to have a woman pay all his bills was a bitch. So I decided to go see Joan Cohn, Harry Cohn's wife. Harry was the head of Columbia. He was a devil of a man, a terrible monster, but I was determined to get my husband back on his feet. I figured I could ask Joan for a favor, to talk to Harry about considering Frank for Maggio. She was very sweet and arranged for me to see Harry myself. So I did. He said to me, 'Oh Christ, he's no actor, he's a singer.' Same thing people said about me, 'She can't act, she's only pretty.' I said, 'Just do me a favor and test him. He's willing to test. And he literally will work for whatever you want to give him.' So he gave him a test and Frank was wonderful. I don't think they paid him more than a thousand dollars a week, but the film was a great success and he got an Oscar for it. Frank was so damn good in it because he didn't take any nonsense and he had a wonderful director, Fred Zinnemann. Frank knew how to take direction."

"What did Frank give you to show his appreciation?" I asked.

"He gave me a little miniature Oscar. But he was no angel, even then. There's another part to that story. He went to Hawaii for that movie and Deborah Kerr was there. I think he got on too well with Miss Kerr. I only found that out later when we were at the Ritz in New York and the elevator man said something to Frank about Deborah Kerr and I said to myself, 'Uh-oh, they've been here together.' Frank could have killed the man. And of course he lied outright to me. I've been married to two of the best liars in the world. Frank would swear that he never slept with another woman. He had three kids with Nancy, but according to Frank, I was the only woman he'd ever been with."

Though Ava claimed that it was she who got Sinatra the part, the more popular story was the one fictionalized in *The Godfather*, which portrayed a crooner down on his luck going to see Don Corleone about a part in a film he desperately wanted. This became the famous scene with the bloody horse's head left in the bed of the movie executive, who swiftly came around after that. Had the Mafia helped Sinatra in such a way?

"That Mafia shit is a lot of crap," Ava said. "We met the Mafia, it was hard not to in our line of business. Especially Frank, who sang in all those nightclubs owned by the Mafia. Frank was supposed to have had a great relationship with Lucky Luciano but I never believed those stories. I really didn't. And I'll tell you something, Larry, there were a lot of stories about me and Frank fighting over these supposed connections of his, but it's an out-and-out lie. We never had a fight about the Mafia. About broads, yes—we had terrible fights."

"How terrible?" I asked.

"Oh, don't get me started. You know who Marilyn Maxwell was?"

"She was 'The Other Marilyn,' wasn't she? Blonde, curvaceous, appeared in a bunch of Bob Hope movies, and was supposedly Hope's mistress."

"Among others," Ava said. "Including Frank. She was actually a sweet, charming girl. Some years after we married, Frank was singing in Atlantic City, and when he was on stage it was sheer electricity. He was incredible to watch. The audience was in the palm of his hand. Women adored him. And he adored women. Seeing Frank in person – there was a magic there that was incomparable. I'd never seen it with anybody else. Maybe Judy Garland or Maria Callas had it. Anyway, I was in the audience, very close to him, and Marilyn Maxwell was there. I swore up and down that he was singing to her, which was completely my imagination. But we had such a battle about that, my God. It went on and on and on. When we got back to New York, at the Hampshire House, I decided to do my thing, which was to run away. That night, I was lucky I wasn't killed. It was after midnight and I ran to Central Park and walked around. It's dangerous now, but it was dangerous then too. And then I decided to take the subway. I really didn't know New York. I used to go there when Bappie was there, but I was always driven places. I didn't know a damn thing about the subway. I stayed on that train for about an hour, or however long it took to get to the end of the line. I had no idea what neighborhood I was in when I got out. And I didn't have a fucking penny. And it was a long way from the Hampshire House. So I walked the streets until I began to get frightened. It was almost daylight when I finally got a taxi and had him drive me back. The driver had picked me up in a pretty scruffy neighborhood, so he thought I was a prostitute. He kept saying, 'Whoever you are going to, I hope you scrunch it, calling a girl out this time of night.' We had a great chat all the way and by the time we got to the Hampshire House the sun had come up. The doorman saw me and said, 'Good morning, Mrs. Sinatra.' I had to ask him to pay the taxi, and then the driver realized who I was. He tried to apologize. I said, 'Don't worry about mistaking me for a whore, you saved my life.'"

I had read this story in Kitty Kelley's book about Sinatra, but she had written that Ava had gone to the airport and flew back to Hollywood. "Oh Christ, no," Ava said. "I was at the end of the subway. I ran away but I sure didn't take a plane. And when I got back, Frank was so relieved to see me, he made me breakfast. He scrambled eggs better than anybody, cooked them with olive oil, stirred them in a very hot pan, slapped them between soft white bread. He made me an egg sandwich and we never discussed it. He was pleased to see that I was okay and I was pleased to be home."

"Fighting with all your husbands must have been exhausting," I said. "Did it ever calm down between you and Frank?"

"Never," Ava said. "I loved him from the very beginning, but he was very jealous, and so was I. And the two men he was most jealous of were Artie Shaw and Howard Hughes. Artie he could deal with because we had been married. But he hated Howard and always insisted that I was fucking him, when I wasn't. And Howard had his people spying on me even when I was married to Artie and to Frank. He was sure I would come around to him in the end. But I never loved Howard. And I never really trusted Frank. Maybe that's why I had those two abortions.

"There was a time when Lana Turner called Frank to ask if she could use the house in Palm Springs, because she had had a terrible fight with her boyfriend. Then Frank and I had one of our terrible fights and this time he ran out, screaming 'I'm going to Palm Springs to fuck Lana Turner'—and he pissed off in my car. We only had one car. I was so fucking angry, I called Bappie and said, 'Pick me up, we're going to Palm Springs.' I drove and we were lucky I didn't kill both of us. But I was going to catch Frank with Lana. We drove around the back of the house and all the curtains were drawn in the bedroom. I climbed over the fence and went to the back door and rang the doorbell. Ben Cole, Lana's business manager, opened the door and I walked in. There was Lana and Frank sitting at the little bar having a drink with Ben. So I joined them, feeling like a fucking fool, and said, 'I thought you'd come down here to fuck Lana.' Lana got furious and got in her car and drove off to some motel. Then Frank decided he was going to find her and fuck her and we had the goddamnest fight I've ever been through. I went to take all my stuff from the house, and Frank grabbed it and threw it into the driveway. Then he called the cops on me. Can you believe that!? The cops came, saw we were having a drunken battle, and tried to get us to calm down. Then Bappie and I drove back home. I'll tell you, Larry, I protected those three bugger husbands of mine for years, trying to be a lady."

The stories Ava told me about the men in her life were only the tip of a very deep iceberg and some of them varied from published accounts that appeared after the fact. But I was hearing Ava's versions and would try to sort them out as we went on. I knew it would take a while to get down all the other wild and crazy stories of her life. I had read that when she and Frank met at David Selznick's house in Palm Springs they went off together in Sinatra's convertible with a fifth of gin and a pistol he kept in his glove compartment and had to pay off the local cops after they were arrested for shooting out the traffic lights and some store windows in Indio. And I read about how Howard Hughes put a prostitute up to sending Ava a letter detailing her dalliances with Sinatra, including a description of his large member which only someone who had seen it could know. (Ava was once asked what she saw in the scrawny 119 pound crooner and responded "His nineteen pounds of cock.") When Ava read that letter she removed the six carat emerald engagement ring Sinatra had given her and threw it out the window of the Hampshire House. She almost cancelled their wedding, but calmed down and went through with it, only to match his roving behavior with affairs of her own during the many months they were separated while she was off making *Mogambo* and *Bhowani Junction* and he was filming *From Here to Eternity* and reviving his singing career on stages in New York and Las Vegas. Their marriage became a farce that was doomed from the start. And weaving in and out of her other romances was the mysterious spymaster, Howard Hughes.

"When I went to Lake Tahoe to finalize my divorce from Frank," Ava said, sadly, about her final marriage mishap, "I invited Luis Miguel Dominguin to join me. He flew in from Spain and we had some drunken nights gambling and fighting. He got angry with me because I wouldn't consent to marry him—Christ, I was just getting divorced!—and threatened to go back to Spain. Well, Howard Hughes had one of his spies watching me. They were always watching me, looking after Howard's interests, even though I hadn't seen Howard in three or four years. But this spy, who was a former cop, saw the battle I was having with Luis Miguel and he went to see him and offered him a special plane to take him back to Madrid. He was out of there in five seconds. That was all Howard's doing. And, of course, Howard appeared the next day. We went out on the lake, which was a sparkling blue, and Howard said, 'You should have a ring the color of this water.' And damn if he didn't pull this perfect Kashmiri sapphire and diamond ring out of a box. It was mine if I consented to marry him. He started telling me how many billions he was worth and how he could buy me the best writers and put me in the biggest movies and we could get a luxurious yacht to travel around the world. He started to cry, telling me how unhappy he was. 'You've been married three times and you're not happy,' he said. 'I could give you anything in the world to make you happy. I can give you the best of everything. I realize you don't love me as you loved the others, but ....' There were tears in his eyes while he was telling me this. Can you believe it? I was there getting a divorce from Frank, whom I still loved but couldn't live with, and here was Luis Miguel and Howard Hughes trying to tie me down again. I just had to laugh. Jesus Christ!

"But Howard wasn't finished with the jewelry. When we left Tahoe we took his plane to Florida, another fiasco. This time it was a diamond necklace he wanted to give me if I fucked him. I found that out from Reenie, who heard it from one of the guys who worked for him. I told Reenie, pack the bags, we're leaving. And we went to Cuba. Without Howard."

As if on cue, the phone rang and Ava picked it up. Mearene Jordan was in the lobby and Ava told her to come up. She was excited to see Reenie, who had come down from Sacramento to see her, and once she poured her a drink she told her friend and confidante that we had been talking about the trip to Tahoe and Florida. "You remember these things better than I do," she said. "Tell Larry what you remember."

"Well," Reenie began, "it started in Tahoe, when Ava decided to fly to Florida. We had to drive to Reno to get Mr. Hughes's plane, so we went in a long train of cars, with Mr. Hughes and Miss G in the lead, me and Glen Brewer, who was part of Mr. Hughes's entertainment staff, behind, with one other guy, and some more cars behind us. Mr. Hughes's men never knew where he was going, because he never bothered to tell anybody anything. The guys that worked for Mr. Hughes were all educated, fine men whom he hired when they came out of college. All they ever did was get him water and ride in cars wondering where they were going. It was hotter than hell, and dusty, and we pulled the gin out. When a car passed us, we all had to stop until the dust settled because Mr. Hughes was allergic to dust. So this half hour ride took two hours.

"It was after 9:00 P.M. when we got to his house in Reno, so we had to wait until the next day to fly out. All his men with all their degrees were sitting around asking, 'Where do you think we're going? I've got to call my wife.' When we finally got to the plane, Mr. Hughes told the pilot to go sit somewhere else because he wanted to fly it. Mr. Hughes didn't take kindly to drinking, but Miss G and I always had a little shopping bag of booze set up, so we would go and take our nip when we wanted."

"I remember sitting in the back and you were in the cockpit with Howard and the other pilot when we were landing in Miami," Ava said.

"That's right. And the other pilot hadn't done a thing, he just sat there the whole trip. We were landing at a military airport and there were all these soldiers there with their guns, and the air controllers in the tower were asking Mr. Hughes to identify himself. This was during the Korean War so there was a lot of concern with security. Mr. Hughes didn't say anything, other than 'Coming in for a landing.' 'Identify yourself!' 'We're coming in for a landing.' 'You'll identify yourself or take a chance on being shot on landing.' Mr. Hughes just ignored them and landed the plane. As he was taxiing up all these soldiers were running toward the plane. He taxied right up to where all these cars were waiting for us and then Mr. Hughes got out of the pilot's seat and told the pilot to sit there. 'If they ask you anything, you tell them nothing,' he instructed the pilot. We kept hearing the controller shouting, 'Identify yourself!' over and over. Mr. Hughes was telling us, 'Let's get ready to go.' And the pilot was saying, 'Mr. Hughes, I'm going to have to tell them something or I'll lose my license.' And Mr. Hughes said, 'Oh, you're not going to lose anything.'"

"The power of the man was shocking," Ava said.

"So we got out of that plane," Reenie continued, "and he and Miss G made a dash for one car and Glen and I were right behind them and then the rest of the PhD's followed us, all into different cars, and we drove to this huge house. Then Mr. Hughes said to me, 'Tomorrow somebody might come, but don't let her in and don't tell her anything.' And sure enough, at 9:00 A.M. the next morning the doorbell rang. This lady was there and asked if she could come in. I said no. She asked why not. I said I had orders not to let anyone in. She asked who gave me the orders. I said I didn't know. She asked who had rented this house. I said I didn't know. She asked if I worked for whoever had rented this house. I said I did and I had come to clean it up. She wanted to know who had hired me. I said I didn't know. She said, 'You're either the smartest nigger I ever met, or the dumbest.'"

"Oh my God," Ava said. "I didn't know this."

"I just stood there and looked at her," Reenie said. "And then I closed the door."

"Did you ever find out who that woman was?"

"She was obviously someone Howard Hughes didn't want to know he was there."

When Ava spoke about the sapphire ring and the diamond necklace she lit another cigarette, blew out the smoke, took a sip of white wine and smiled at me. "I could be a very lovely lady if I had that jewelry today," she said.

"But you have to be a certain person to accept things for things," Reenie said. "And you're not that type of person."

"I threw that ring back at him," Ava said. "But he kept us sitting in that airport all day when we tried to go to Havana."

"That's because you were leaving without him," Reenie said.

"Damn right I was, after what his man said to you about the necklace," she reminded Reenie. "And also because Howard kept saying we were going to Argentina to see Peron, with whom he had some crooked deal, I'm sure, and then kept putting it off while we kept sitting around day after day. Screw Howard Hughes!"

Cuba? Argentina? Juan Peron? We were just in Tahoe, Reno and Miami. My head was beginning to swim. Was all this happening with Ava over a period of days? Was her life this chaotic?

"No, the Argentina thing wasn't then," Reenie said. "That was another time. But it was during that period. When we started from Palm Springs."

"You mean when we made the famous trip down to Mexico?"

'Yeah, right. Right. But how we happened to go back to Florida with Mr. Hughes, I don't know."

"Might have been a stop off, on our way to Argentina."

"No," Reenie corrected. "Argentina was an afterthought. We were going to Nassau, remember? We went in the amphibian plane and we stopped in Key West where they wanted to know who was in the plane and Mr. Hughes insisted that we all had to change our names. Everybody, from the biggest down. That's when we came up with Ann Clark for you."

"Right," Ava said, remembering. "I wonder what Howard used?"

"I don't remember, but when we were landing in Nassau, he wouldn't dare go into the regular airport. He said we were going to stay at Harry Oakes place. Harry Oakes was the richest man in the Bahamas and had been mysteriously killed in the forties. So Mr. Hughes flew in the back way and landed the plane on the water in back of the Oakes estate. The workers came out in three boats and took us to the house, so we never went through customs. I'd never seen anything like it except in the movies. And my job was to pack and unpack. That's all I ever did when we traveled with Mr. Hughes, because you never knew how long you were going to be anywhere."

Listening to these two women reminisce I realized that it was nearly impossible to get to the end of any story. They had lived adventurous lives in glamorous cities around the world. Men were forever chasing after Ava, she was forever getting bored with her lovers, and trying to get her story straight was truly a challenge. "Can we back up for a moment?" I interrupted. "Before the Bahamas, you mentioned that Howard kept you from flying to Cuba. How did he do that?"

"All the planes were grounded," Ava said, "there were no planes flying out when we got there. There was no way that every plane to Havana was stopped all day long without some explanation. All they told us was that the planes to Cuba had been cancelled. And then his man Glen showed up and tried to talk us into not leaving. I told him to tell his boss that I was leaving because I was bored sitting around that house. I was a young girl, I wanted to go out, do things, and all we did was sit around his house eating buttered steaks and ice cream with caramel sauce, because that's what Howard liked to eat. With peas and a salad, no potatoes, no vegetables."

"But they were gorgeous steaks," Reenie beamed.

"And do you remember the time Hep climbed on the kitchen table and ate all the steaks and butter?" Ava laughed. "Oh that was funny."

Hep was one gift Howard Hughes had given her when they first met, before her marriage to Artie Shaw, and she had accepted it. He was a Belgian shepherd dog. "He was a magnificent creature," Ava said, "with a hokey name, Hep. Those were the days of 'being hep' and all that jazz. I was living in a little house in Hollywood and Howard said the dog has got to be 'as beautiful and perfect as you.' Well, I must say, he was beautiful. He was a gentle, sweet, loving dog. Then, a few years later after I married Artie and moved into his house on Bedford Drive, Hep had to live outside because Artie had a couple working for him who had a small dog. Hep had always been accustomed to sleeping on my bed and suddenly he was thrown out to the garden. I was working in those days and Hep learned how to scale this six-foot wall and run away. He always ran through the Wilshire Blvd. traffic to the same house. He had a tag on his collar, and the people would bring him back home. I got to know them quite well. And one day they telephoned me and said that Hep was there. So I went to fetch him. They had a 16-year-old son who was very bright but had a muscular disease, so he was spastic. When I got there he had a seizure and kicked his slipper across the room. Hep picked up the slipper and brought it back to him." The memory made Ava cry. "I can take talking about people, but my animals…oh God." She continued to cry for a while. "I gave him the dog. He was happy there. He wasn't happy where he was."

"That Howard Hughes," Reenie said. "He really tried for you. Too bad the chemistry wasn't right."

"Watch it," Ava said. "You're sounding like Bappie. I'll never forget when she went to help Howard after he blackened my eye and I hit him with that brass bell. If she could have sold me to him, she would have. I'm sorry to say that about my sister, but it would have been so. Until this day, she regrets that I didn't marry him, because she would have been better off, you see? But I didn't love him, so why would I marry him? People say that Bappie had such control over my life—she had no control whatsoever. I did what I wanted to do, not what Bappie wanted. Because otherwise I might have been a whore."

"Nonsense," Reenie said. "No such thing. I think Bappie wanted you to be with Howard because of her feelings for Charlie."

Charlie Guest was Hughes's personal secretary. Bappie had fallen for him when Ava was married to Artie Shaw. "Poor Charlie," Ava said. "Bappie really loved him. So did Howard. He had been a pro golfer and a jazz musician before he worked for Howard. He was a very handsome man, but he was a dreadful alcoholic. Died of cirrhosis of the liver. The last few years Howard had him into all sorts of cures. In those days you didn't talk about it. It was like sex; you did it but you didn't discuss it.

"We took a trip to New York with Howard, Bappie and Charlie, and that was the first time Charlie was hospitalized for his liver thing. From then on, it was all downhill. He just sat at home and drank. Howard wouldn't let him drive because it was too dangerous, so his car was taken from him. They didn't give him any cash, so he couldn't buy whiskey. It was cruel, actually, a terrible thing to do to the poor man. But he would still somehow get booze. He was a gin drinker. Howard stopped trusting him. He should have trusted him more than those Mormons who probably did him in.

"I saw Charlie have a seizure once—horrible experience. The eyes go back, the spasms, the terrible pain. We had to send him off to the hospital that night. Then I got a job doing a film in Italy and Bappie went with me. While we were gone poor Charlie got very, very drunk in their house, which was near mine in Nichols Canyon, and he went outside, had another seizure, and died. Bappie wasn't there when he died."

"She felt guilty about that," Reenie said. "It colored her feelings towards Mr. Hughes, because he wanted you so much. She just wasn't seeing the Howard Hughes you saw."

"Look," Ava said, "I know Howard could be charming, and I don't think he was deliberately unkind, but a lot of his attitude toward his factory workers was unkind. There wasn't one Jew or one black who worked for the Hughes Tool Company. They had nothing to do with Howard. He would never see them; they would never be in his presence. I find that highly unkind and downright fucking cruel."

"Did you watch him at work?" I wondered.

"He did all his business at night, on the phone, talking to lawyers and the people who worked for him. He would wake his people up in the middle of the night and if they didn't like it, he'd fire them. That's what he did with Noah Dietrich, his right hand man and business advisor. He'd call him at two, three o'clock in the morning and give him orders. When Dietrich married his third wife, who had two young daughters, she didn't appreciate the calls and insisted he tell Howard to call during office hours. Howard asked him if that was his final word, and the next morning Dietrich didn't have a job. No more private plane, no more yacht, everything was snatched overnight. Dietrich wrote a book about it. But that was exactly who Howard was."

"So how come you let him hang around for fifteen years?" I asked. "If it wasn't his money or his expensive presents, and you felt he was a racist, were you keeping him hanging because he made all your other men jealous? Or was he just an amusement that you couldn't let go?"

"He was amusing, hon. He loved music, classical and jazz. I told you that he loved to dance. But I hated dancing with him because he held me too tight, and he was a lousy dancer. So were Artie and Frank; neither could keep time at all. Mickey was a great dancer. I once danced with Fred Astaire at Gregory Peck's house. Greg was the worst dancer in the world; he couldn't keep his feet out of the way. But dancing with Fred Astaire was like dancing with Nureyev. I couldn't keep time! I was too in awe."

"When did it finally end with Howard Hughes?"

"In 1956 or '57. I was renting some place. Howard called and asked if he could come by. I told him my sister Myra was visiting and he said he'd love to meet her. It became a very weird night. We were going out to the Beachcomber. Howard came and picked us up. We went out to his car, I got in the front, Myra and Bappie in back, and we waited for Howard to get in. And we waited…and waited…and waited. Howard didn't appear. I thought, 'Well, this is a little too long,' although it would be just like Howard to do something like that. I thought maybe he went to take a pee in the bushes. Eventually, I got out and went to the back of the car and he was lying there. He had slipped and fallen and hit his head on the bumper. He had probably slipped on his shoelace because he never laced his shoes. My sisters got out and we all picked him up. He had a terrible bump on his head, so we went back into the house and put a bandage on his head. Yet he still insisted on going to the Beachcomber, so we got it together and went. And that night he told me he was going to marry Jean Peters unless I agreed to marry him. I suppose that was his last appeal. And it was the last time I saw Howard, who married her right after that."

7

A Real-Life Contessa, Hurtfully Wounded

HUGHES MARRIED JEAN PETERS in January 1957, the same year Ava moved out of the country. She went to Rome to film *The Naked Maja*, about the artist Francisco Goya and his nude model of the title. She also wanted to renew her on-again-off-again affair with Walter Chiari, who admitted to being obsessed with her since they first met while filming *The Barefoot Contessa* two years earlier. She then went to Mexico for *The Sun Also Rises*; and to Spain to try her hand at sticking a *banderilla* from horseback into a young bull, but fell from the horse and bruised her face. She found an apartment near Madrid and made Spain her home until 1968, when she moved to London. In 1959 she went to Australia to film *On the Beach*. The Hollywood hassles and media harassment were behind her. She had three failed marriages, none of which lasted even two years, and an endless parade of actors, writers, doctors, businessmen, soldiers, musicians, singers, and bullfighters who pursued her. She found, in Spain, the nightlife and attitude that fit her freewheeling spirit. And that was best expressed dancing the flamenco.

In 1980 I went to Florida to interview the novelist James A. Michener and developed a friendship with him that lasted until his death seventeen years later. When I told him that I was seeing Ava, Jim wrote me this letter.

"One night during Madrid's San Isidro festivities after the seventh or eighth bullfight, I left a party at which Orson Welles was holding forth, and he was never in better form, trying to convince me that his favorite matador, Curro Romero was one of the best ever. I knew Romero had been good in his prime, but in later years he gave appalling performances from which the police had to rescue him lest the fans kill him in disgust. Consequently, Welles did not sway me, and he dismissed me as beyond salvation.

"A troupe of us then trailed off, without Welles, to a gala party graced by Ava Gardner, who was delicately inebriated, marvelously amusing, and attentive like the rest of us to the two beautiful female flamenco dancers who danced nude, to the accompaniment of a dazzling guitarist with a whiskey voice admirably suited to his music and the clacking of the castanets.

"Ava was extremely beautiful, a real-life Contessa, and yet hurtfully wounded in ways I could not fathom. She was grand but she was fading and the combination was haunting, one of the veritable items in a shifting, shadowy world.

"She had been getting some bad press and when I had the opportunity I presented myself to her as an American writer who thought she had been unfairly treated and that she had handled herself magnificently. She looked at me through misty eyes and asked who I was. 'James Michener,' I said.

"'And what do your friends call you, James?' she asked.

"'Jim.'

"'Well, fuck off, Jim.'"

And how did Michener react? "I laughed then, and I laugh now, because I forgive actors any excesses since theirs is a tougher ballgame than I have to play. It's the most grueling profession in the world."

I asked Ava if she remembered this. She didn't, but she didn't refute it. "Sounds like me," she said. "There were a lot of drunken flamenco nights."

"Why'd you leave Spain?" I asked.

"Because it changed so terribly. I just got tired of dancing the flamenco. When I first decided to settle down there I bought a Mercedes convertible and drove from France into Spain, to San Sebastian on the sea. I was with a publicist friend of mine and we decided to take a swim. He wore swimming trunks and I had on a two-piece bathing suit, long before bikinis. The bottom went up to my waist and the bra was too big, so I was well covered. A Civil Guard appeared and was ready to arrest us because we were underdressed. He said a man in his trunks and a woman in a two-piece bathing suit were not allowed. Another time I went to a bullfight with a little sunback dress that went not even to the bra line in the back. Again, a Civil Guard approached the man I was with and said in Spanish, 'Please explain to the senorita that it's not her fault for wearing the dress, it's the fault of the men behind her who have such foul minds.' So I had to put a scarf on. Today in Spain everybody is naked on the beach. But in those days, they were dead serious. In Franco's time, if you smoked marijuana you could land in jail for a year. They were serious about drugs. Now it's wide open."

"When was the last time you were in Spain?"

"About two years ago I did a movie for television called *Harem* with Omar Sharif. It was a piece of rubbish. We went on location to Cordova and Seville, where we stayed at the beautiful Alfonso Hotel. The minute I got there they told me, 'Don't go out alone after dark.' It was too dangerous, they said. The thieves were all on drugs. People were mugged, killed, cars were broken into, and luggage and passports were stolen. The tourist spots in the south of Spain were the worst places to go. It was pretty sad."

Roddy McDowall, one of Ava's close friends, stopped by her hotel while I was there and the two Hollywood war horses fell right in, chatting about their mutual friends, sharing gossip and illnesses, and going down memory lane. McDowall was just thirteen when he first saw Ava in 1942 and he asked her for an autograph. A teenager herself, Ava signed it "Mrs. Mickey Rooney." Thirty years later McDowall directed Ava in

The Ballad of Tam-Lin, a film very few saw and even fewer remember. As a child actor, McDowall appeared in *My Friend Flicka, How Green Was My Valley*, and *Lassie Come Home*. As an adult, he was perhaps best known for playing Cornelius and Caesar in four *Planet of the Apes* movies. When Ava mentioned that I was working with her on her memoir, McDowall started rattling off names of people I should talk to: Lauren Bacall, Elizabeth Taylor, Stephanie Powell, Sidney Guilaroff, Dirk Bogarde, Bill Tupple....

"Get them before we lose them," he told me. Then, addressing Ava, he said, "You haven't seen yet what Dirk Bogarde wrote about you in my second *Double Exposure* book." McDowall had published his first book of star photographs in 1966. "Dirk said, 'She is the only woman I know who can still a crowded room merely by entering it....Her presence is a reminder that beauty still walks the land.' So true, Ava."

"Oh please," Ava laughed. "The other day Larry and I were in the lobby of this hotel and a photographer asked me to step out of his picture. Some reminder."

"Well, weren't you the lucky one," McDowall said. "Do you realize if he recognized you what that picture might have been worth?"

"That's what Larry said. Lucky me, with my arm glued to my body and my unrecognizable face."

"Have you any awareness of the amount of affection that all these people I mentioned have for you?" McDowall said, trying to lift her spirits. "Bill Tupple, the head of makeup at MGM, said the three most beautiful women he ever worked with are you, Hedy Lamarr, and Elizabeth Taylor."

"And what about Garbo?" Ava asked.

"Garbo didn't have good skin tone, she had dozens of freckles. Her bone structure was wonderful, but she wasn't as beautiful as you."

"Darling," Ava stopped him, "she was *Garbo*. She was what you saw on the screen."

"Do you remember the letter I read to you from Louise Brooks?" McDowall asked. "The one that made you cry?" Then he turned to me and explained. "Louise Brooks, silent movie star, beautiful woman, a heavy alcoholic who missed the last twenty years of her life and had never seen Ava until I brought her a television and she caught one of Ava's movies. She said she identified with her screen spirit. She felt Ava's spirit was transcendental and that she had an essence of simplicity and opulence. Which is true. But of course, Ava doesn't know it because she knows nothing about herself."

"Ha!" said Ava. "Ha!"

"It's true," McDowall said to Ava. "You rather liked not being able to work. You've never wanted to work, because you've always been petrified of acting. You were afraid of everything because of how they used you as a commodity in your early days. You have absolutely no knowledge of how good you are. No knowledge of the depths of your intellect or your talent."

"That's true. I can't speak properly, I can't photograph properly, I'm always chewing on my jaws, and I had to get drunk before I went to work in the morning."

"I've often wondered what would have happened if your acting career had been spent consistently with directors like John Huston and George Cukor."

"Well, for them I really applied myself."

"And I wonder what would have happened if you had been permitted by MGM to play the maid in that play in La Jolla."

"Oh my goodness, yes. That was quite a famous play. Gregory Peck and I had just done *The Great Sinner* at Metro and Greg came to me one day and asked if I'd ever been in the theater. I told him that was too terrifying. He said, 'What if you did something small, and I'd be there with you?' He gave me this play and I read it and thought, okay, I'll try it. I was young then; I wasn't so absolutely terrified as I was later. And it was a small part, not the lead. So Greg said we should go see the big wigs in the executive building at Metro to see if they'd allow it. We did, and I was told no. I had to either play the lead or nothing. And I wasn't even a big star then. It would have been a wonderful experience and I might have taken an interest in acting. Who knows?"

"The problem with you, Ava," McDowall said, "is that you say things about yourself that are mind-boggling to those who know you. Part of the reason you've always been so wildly effective in movies is because of your power of concentration. It's almost childlike. Your investment in the moment is complete. That's coupled with something else which you don't understand: the margin of your charisma. But nobody ever really sees themselves as others see them. Bette Davis doesn't understand at all that thing that she has. And you don't understand at all what it is. Your mystique is a constant, it doesn't matter what the material is, it's always there."

"Probably why I turned down so many good roles," Ava said. "I didn't understand the margin of my charisma."

"You're mocking me," McDowall said. "But it's true. Do you regret turning down those pictures?"

"Good God yes," Ava said soberly. "Now I'm sorry, because some of them were extremely good, and paid very good money at the time. I should have done *Sweet Bird of Youth*, *The Graduate*, and *Love Me or Leave Me*, the Ruth Etting story that Doris Day did with James Cagney. I went on suspension not to do that. There were other really good things that I should have done. But there you go. I did *Tam Lin*—and they cut it to pieces after they took it out of your hands."

"Don't remind me," McDowall said. "But even there, I remember how petrified you were when you had to dress down all the young actors in that scene at the end of the film, where you walked up the staircase, turned and had to deliver a tirade of very difficult structured dialogue."

"And I couldn't do it because I loved those kids. How could I yell at them?"

"And I said to you, 'Remember those nights when you used to come home pissed in Spain and threw people out in the morning? Pretend it's like that.' And you did it."

"There were a lot of pissed-off nights in Spain to recall," Ava smiled.

"And at the end of the film, I still get goose bumps. When you had to say to Ian McShane, 'I give you one week and after that I'm going to hunt you down.' We shot it in close-up. McShane says you're going to die and you say 'I will not die.' Your eyes filled up and it showed what an incredible actress you were."

"Well," Ava said, bringing the conversation to the present, "that's what happened in the hospital. I refused to die. I refused to lie in bed and sit in a wheelchair. I guess I'm a survivor."

McDowall compressed his forehead in all seriousness and asked Ava about her condition. But Ava said she had already told me all about it in detail, so he could read about it after she died.

"When are you planning to do that?" McDowall asked.

"I'm as good as dead already," Ava replied.

"You just said you're a survivor."

"I am, my dear. But for how long?" And then she changed the subject. "Do you remember the night we had dinner in that little restaurant with Princess Margaret and Noel Coward in London?"

"Noel adored you," McDowall said, glad to have something more uplifting to talk about.

"I used to visit him when he was sick," Ava said. "What a wonderful man."

"Did you see the documentary Marlene Dietrich did with Maximilian Schell?" McDowall asked. "It's all about her, and she isn't even in it! It's great! You hear her and you keep thinking you're going to see her. It's a wonderful manipulation."

"And she's completely removed," Ava said.

"Maximilian told me that in her old age Dietrich has reverted to speaking in slum German, the equivalent of cockney English."

"She talks constantly."

"I spoke to her about two months ago. She's very suspicious. What's interesting about that documentary is that she has forgotten her truths. She said she doesn't have a sister, but she does. She wrote a book that was only printed in Germany. The book is about how she taught Von Sternberg to direct and Hemingway to write. Her child is obviously immaculately conceived because there isn't anything about the extraordinary sexual life that she lived."

"She wrote me a letter when she was tangled up with this writer who was writing about her. She thought I knew him and was going to talk about her, but I didn't, and I wouldn't."

Ava said she adored Dietrich as an actress. I asked her who else she adored and she mentioned Jean Harlow, Joan Crawford, Greta Garbo, Katharine Hepburn, Clark Gable, Gregory Peck, and Jane

Fonda. When I asked her if Paul Newman was the only actor she didn't care for, she added two others, Kirk Douglas and John Wayne. And then she told us a funny story about how her sister Bappie once dropped her off at George Cukor's house and then had a flat tire in front of Katharine Hepburn's house. Hepburn came out and changed the tire for her. "Howard Hughes had quite a love affair with Katharine Hepburn," Ava said. "She had great admiration for him. There were a lot of women in his life, my God." McDowall had a few Hepburn stories to tell and Ava said she had met her once at a Cukor dinner and "very carefully called her Miss Hepburn."

McDowall said he had been watching a few of the Elvis Presley movies on TV and Ava responded that she had seen some while at the hospital. "Elvis and Marilyn Monroe," Ava said, "they truck them out every year at their birthdays and continue to write crap about them. What tragic lives. Marilyn just took too many pills trying to get a good night's sleep. She and Elvis Presley, they won't let them die and stay dead in peace."

"Well, Miss G," McDowall said, "it's time for me to make my exit. Just make sure this young man talks to the people in this town who know and love you."

When we were alone I asked Ava if there were any athletes that she had ever had a crush on and she said there was one—Sandy Koufax. "I love baseball, and I loved the way he pitched. I wrote a fan letter to him when I was in Spain—sent him a telegram, actually. But I goofed and sent it on Rosh Hashanah, the Jewish Day of Atonement. So that wasn't very smart."

I told her that I knew someone who knew Koufax and if she still wanted his autograph I could probably arrange it. "Would you?" Ava said. "Could you get me a photograph?"

It made me smile, this famous woman getting excited by the thought of getting a signed picture of a baseball hero from her past. I wondered what Sandy Koufax would think when my friend made the request. He was a shy, reluctant star, just like Ava. And it only took a phone call and a two day wait before Koufax asked where to send it.

On February 25, Jess Morgan called to say that Ava was ready to make a deal with me. Up until this time we hadn't talked business, and that was okay with me. I was hoping to put this off for as long as possible, because I needed to finish writing *The Hustons*. But I could see that Ava wasn't well enough to wait another six or eight months. She wanted to return to her flat in London, and she wanted me to follow. "I can't stay here," Ava had said the week before. "I've got to see my dog. He talked to me this morning. We had a chat. I'd travel a hell of a lot more if I could bring him along, but he can't stand being quarantined."

"She wants at least a million dollars," Morgan told me. "So that means I won't accept anything less than a million and a quarter, which will guarantee you $250,000. And anything more than that, she will split with you 80-20."

"Jess," I said, "you know I'm working on *The Hustons* now."

"I know, Larry. But I also know that Ava has been looking for someone to work with for years, and she's not well. She's had other writers and they haven't worked out."

"So what are you suggesting?"

"To make this deal. You'll figure out a way to make it happen."

But I couldn't figure out a way. I was too deeply into the other book, having interviewed 200 people for it, and though I was all right spending weekends with Ava, I just couldn't see putting what I was doing aside to go live in London for the next six months, which is what I thought it might take to get her story down.

Ava was not pleased. She and I didn't talk about it. Everything now came through Morgan. We had spent four weekends together and I felt that we had just scratched the surface. Every story she told me could be enhanced. There were all her movies we didn't get to, all the coworkers, all those flamenco nights, all the other men and women in her life, all her memories still to tap. Al Pacino might have been right when he said Ava was worth more than Huston, but my head was with John, Walter, Anjelica, Tony, Danny and the incredible cast of characters in their lives. Theirs was a rich and diverse family saga that spanned over a hundred years. Ava Gardner was still a spirit I'd yet to capture, a fantasy I needed to turn real. I liked being with her, and I wish we could have continued our weekend talks, but when it came time to choose, I really had no choice. If she hadn't suffered that stroke she might have been less concerned about time; but she knew her days were numbered, and she was right. She died of pneumonia on Jan 25, 1990, less than two years after I last saw her. She was just 67 years old.

The sky over England turned black and the wind howled on the day Ava died. Over a million trees were uprooted and 47 people lost their lives to the hurricane that would be known as The Burns Day Storm, one of the most severe storms that ever hit the U.K. How ironic, I thought, for such a natural force to roar on the same day such a human force was silenced. She was such a unique nihilist, such a fantastic iconoclast, and such an extraordinary hedonist. I had a few incredible weekends listening to her reflect on her life and each time I left her, I looked forward to seeing her again, hearing more of her stories, asking her new questions, and taking advantage of the opportunity she presented to me like a gift. For that is what she was: a gift. She was a woman who danced, drank and smoked her way through many lives and numerous worlds; she understood and inspired great talent; she had entered into scenes far more exotic and emotional than any she had played on the screen and had come through them all the wiser. She was a survivor.

When Nick Nolte once asked Robert Mitchum why he had spurned her advances during the filming of *My Forbidden Past*, Mitchum said, "She was too addictive."

Mickey Rooney, Artie Shaw, John Huston, George C. Scott, Frank Sinatra, Luis Miguel Dominguin, Howard Hughes and so many others who fell under her spell knew only too well what Mitchum meant.

The Films of Ava Gardner

We Were Dancing (1942)
Joe Smith—American (1942)
Sunday Punch (1942)
This Time for Keeps (1942)
Kid Glove Killer (1942)
Pilot No. 5 (1943)
Hitler's Madman (1943)
Ghosts On the Loose (1943)
Young Ideas (1943)
The Lost Angel (1943)
Swing Fever (1943)
Three Men in White (1944)
Maisie Goes to Reno (1944)
She Went to the Races (1945)
Whistle Stop (1946)
The Killers (1946)
The Hucksters (1947)
Singapore (1947)
One Touch of Venus (1948)

The Bribe (1949)
The Great Sinner (1949)
East Side, West Side (1949)
My Forbidden Past (1951)
Pandora and the Flying Dutchman (1951)
Show Boat (1951)
Lone Star (1952)
The Snows of Kilimanjaro (1952)
Ride, Vaquero! (1953)
The Band Wagon (1953)
Mogambo (1953)
Knights of the Round Table (1954)
The Barefoot Contessa (1954)
Bhowani Junction (1954)
The Little Hut (1954)
The Sun Also Rises (1957)
The Naked Maja (1959)
On the Beach (1959)
The Angel Wore Red (1960)
55 Days at Peking (1963)
Seven Days in May (1964)
The Night of the Iguana (1964)
The Bible (...In the Beginning) (1966)
Mayerling (1969)
The Ballad of Tam Lin (1972)
The Life and Times of Judge Roy Bean (1972)
Earthquake (1974)
Permission to Kill (1974)
The Blue Bird (1976)

The Cassandra Crossing (1977)
The Sentinel (1977)
City on Fire (1979)
The Kidnapping of the President (1980)
Priest of Love (1981)

Lawrence Grobel (www.lawrencegrobel.com) is a novelist, journalist, biographer, poet and teacher. Four of his 22 books have been singled out as Best Books of the Year by *Publisher's Weekly* and many have appeared on Best Seller lists. He is the recipient of a National Endowment for the Arts Fellowship for his fiction. PEN gave his *Conversations with Capote* a Special Achievement Award. The French Society of Film Critics awarded his *Al Pacino* their Prix Litteraire as the Best International Book of 2008. James A. Michener called his biography, *The Hustons*, "a masterpiece." His *The Art of the Interview* is used as a text in many journalism schools. *Writer's Digest* called him "a legend among journalists." Joyce Carol Oates dubbed him "The Mozart of Interviewers" and *Playboy* singled him out as "The Interviewer's Interviewer" after publishing his interviews with Barbra Streisand, Dolly Parton, Henry Fonda and Marlon Brando. He has written for dozens of magazines and has been a Contributing Editor for *Playboy*, *Movieline*, *World (*New Zealand), and *Trendy* (Poland). He served in the Peace Corps, teaching at the Ghana Institute of Journalism; created the M.F.A. in Professional Writing for Antioch University; and taught in the English Department at UCLA for ten years. He has appeared on CNN, *The Today Show, Good Morning America, The Charlie Rose Show* and in two documentaries, *Salinger* and Al Pacino's *Wilde Salome*. His books can be found at Amazon.com. He is married to the artist Hiromi Oda and they have two daughters.

Ten Days on Brando's Island

From *Conversations with Brando* by Lawrence Grobel

June 13: Day One

I'm sitting next to Marlon's Tahitian wife, Tarita, in the small twin-engine plane that's taking us to Brando's island. We're flying into thick gray clouds, and Tarita is frightened. She thinks we should turn back. Dick Johnson, Marlon's accountant, reassures her. "I called the island," he says, "it's not raining there."

Suddenly the sun is gone and rain pelts the plane's windows. Tarita clutches her seven-year old daughter, Cheyenne. The pilot flies through the storm. Below us is Tetiaroa: thirteen small flat islets, each covered with palm trees, arranged around a turquoise lagoon. We land on the airstrip of the only island that's inhabited. The plane taxis the width of the island and stops a few yards from Marlon's bungalow.

Brando is waiting. He kisses Tarita on both cheeks, and then comes to greet me. He is wearing an Indian cotton hooded shirt and pants, and with his gray-white hair, paunch, and wry, warm smile he has the appearance of an East Indian holy man. He jokes about his outfit, which he says he designed because he is prone to sunstroke and must keep covered. He takes my bag and leads me to a thatched roof bungalow. Everything but the cement floor in the octagonal room is made from palm trees. Brando comments on my sandals that, he says, will not last because sand will get between my toes and the leather.

"You can tell a man's education by the spread of his toes," he says, making one of the seemingly random remarks that pepper his conversation. He puts his own bare feet on the windowsill. "If the toes are widespread, they grew up shoeless," he says, and then he proceeds to launch into a discourse on the nature of Tahitians. For two hours, he talks—of primitive tribes "looking through two thousand years of history with ballpoint pens through their noses," of the Untouchables in India, American blacks, Haitians, Africans, Japanese, Pakistanis, Polynesians.

He talks about his ambitions for his island. He'd like to build a school for the blind here and invite oceanographers to come and conduct experiments. He's had forty scientists and a Japanese archaeologist check the land and he's had aerial photographs taken. But he's had to curtail the various projects because things tend to fall apart when he's gone. "You can't bring culture here, you have to adapt to theirs," he says, swiping at some annoying flies, catching two in his hand. And Tahitians, he says, do not have goals or ambitions. "Nothing bothers them, if they have flies, they live with them. The flies breed in the fallen coconuts, and unless you go around picking up all the coconuts you can't get rid of them. But tell a Tahitian that and he doesn't believe it."

He is impressed with the Tahitians' ability to read body language. "They can appear as if they aren't paying attention but they can remember if you wore socks or not, if your pants were clean, the color of your shoes."

Most people who come down, he says, get bored after a few weeks. You have to find yourself, your inner resources. "When I first get here I'm like a discharged battery. It takes a few weeks to unwind, but eventually the island's slower rhythms sink in." He has stayed up to six months at one time. His shortest stay was three days. "When people come here to see me, they're usually all wound up, they talk fast, they've got projects, ideas, deals. And I sit here like a whale."

A cool wind blows through the windows. The bungalow is close to the water's edge. Directly across the lagoon is another island. There are pigs on that one, he says. He'd like to bring over some wild animals—elephants, gorillas. But he's concerned they'd be neglected when he's gone. "Must bring up animals like a child."

I ask him about his children's education. He prefers to keep Teihotu and Cheyenne in Tahiti, where they can learn to enjoy life and nature. He doesn't approve of the peer pressure in America. "Teenagers are the most conformists of people. They are anything but radical. You've got to learn the right words, dress the right way."

He asks if I'm hungry and we take a walk to his bungalow. He points out the plants growing in the sand in front of his door, which he says he waters with his urine. I notice the tall antenna in front of his hut, which he had built "out of rage because the phones are so bad." Inside, there are two double beds, shelves of books and cassettes, a bottle of Rolaids, packages of grape Double Bubble sugarless gum. Researching *Apocalypse Now* he read a stack of books which all told the same story: how our being there was all for gain, what Vietnam had was rubber, oil, raw materials. "All the bullshit and propaganda about freedom—hogwash."

He shows me his ham radio, which must constantly be "cooked" to keep away the mildew. He sits down and twirls the dial. Foreign music and languages come over the radio. "That's China, their anthem… that's Mexico…that's Cuba."

The flies continue to bother him. He slaps at one that lands on him, swipes at others that fly by. His hands are as fast as a lizard's tongue. "If you could take all the time you spend poised to catch flies and put it together you'd have a pretty neat vacation," he observes. Brando says he was once influenced by the Jain philosophy, which holds that one shouldn't kill anything, not even a fly. He says it made sense for a while, until he thought it through—and realized how, with every breath you take, you're killing something.

His accountant, Dick, the island foreman, William, and Tarita come by to discuss island business. I get up and Marlon tells me to feel free to explore the island. "I'll come by later," he says. "We can watch the sun set. There's sometimes a touch of green just as it drops."

Along the beach I watch hand-sized crabs crawling along the sand in their shells. Palm sprouts grow out of fallen coconuts. Palm trees curved according to how the wind was blowing when they were growing. An abundance of coral, shells, black sea cucumbers, at the bottom of the clear water. Gentle lapping of the water on the shore. Lush clouds, blue sky, discarded radio batteries.

The wind begins to blow. Rain comes and goes. In my toilet, a large cockroach floats.

Dinner. Marlon comes to get me. We are joined by Dick, Brando's secretary, Caroline, and her six-year-old daughter. The dining room has twenty tables, nineteen of them empty. We eat meat, potatoes, fish, salad, ice cream, fruit, and cheese. Marlon says he's on a diet so he doesn't eat the bread. He asks me if I ever saw *Mondo Cane*. Tells a story of a woman in Hong Kong who brought her toy poodle to a restaurant and the waiter took it, cooked it, and fed it to her. We laugh. Marlon is entertaining, expressive. Laments that he can't remember things. Picks up a place mat and says there are ways to remember, if you had connecting stories for each line in the place mat.

After dinner, Marlon and I walk out on the short, narrow pier. He says he'd like to build a lifting hydraulic patio on the pier that would work on the principle of the wind. It could raise you twenty feet and lower you when the wind died down. Explains how transmitters work, how humpback whales can be heard singing for five hundred miles. He's full of random bits of arcane knowledge.

Walking back he picks off a small white flower from a tree and says, "Smell this. You can sometimes smell the island before you see it because of these."

From a bungalow, I hear the sound of television. Tarita and other Tahitians are watching. Marlon prefers silence, but he's made the concession. TV brought the Twist to Tahiti in twenty minutes, he says.

June 14: Day Two

Brando is tied up with island business: developing tourism, building a house on the other side of the island, supervising new construction of a reception area, having roofs re-thatched. He's in conflict over tourists coming to his island. He's tired of having them snap pictures of him and at one point closed down the hotel and fired thirty-five people. But for tax purposes, and because it's expensive to keep pouring money into the island, he has reopened it for one-and two-day tours. Because there is a limited amount of water, tourism can never fully develop. "He'll always be losing money," Dick tells me.

I walk around the island, snorkel, and swim on the other side which opens into a magnificent bay.

In the evening Marlon and I take a walk, stretch out on the sand, and talk for three hours. He is eloquent, passionate, and outrageous. "That star next to the moon is always there," he says, looking up at the night sky. "I remember I was in Marrakech on a sparkling, crystalline desert night and I saw the same star. I'd been talking to this girl a long time—it was four in the morning—and the muezzin came out on his minaret and started chanting. It was an enchanted moment. It made me feel like I was in Baghdad in the twelfth century." I ask him if the girl he was with was a Moslem. "Nah," he says, "airline hostess."

He then changes the subject to American Indians. Says some Indians hate him because he's white. He talks of hustling, and how he's never promoted himself or his movies. Even a writer like Saul Bellow, he complains, goes on TV to hustle his work just like everybody else. Brando also speaks of poets he likes, Dylan Thomas and Kenneth Patchen, and quotes one of Patchen's small poems:

Wait   wait

    wait   wait

        now.

I bring up T. S. Eliot's "The Love Song of J. Alfred Prufrock" and he says, "If the mermaids can't sing for me here, Christ, they never will."

June 15: Day Three

"My favorite interview," Marlon is saying, "was on television with Mrs. Arnold Palmer. The interviewer asked, 'Is there any special ritual that you go through before your husband plays?' She says, `No.' `Nothing at all?' `Well, I kiss his balls.' The interviewer did a double take. 'You mean his golf balls, right?' `Of course,' Mrs. Palmer said, 'what did you think I meant?' "

I was hoping this was a prelude to our sitting down with the tape recorder on, but Marlon's got another day of island meetings before we can begin. "I'm not business-oriented," he says. "I could have been a multimillionaire but then I would have had to have been that kind of a person, and I'm not." He adds that if *Superman* is as big a hit as they say it's going to be he'll make a lot of money because he's got a percentage. (According to Dick Johnson, when Marlon finished shooting *Superman*, for which he was paid between $2 and $3 million, he returned to Tetiaroa and said to Dick, "Twelve days work, cash on the line, who's worth that kind of money?" "Nobody I know," Dick answered.)

Before dinner I join Marlon at the bar. His meetings are over; Dick has flown back to Papeete. The bartender is a German named George who has floated around Tahiti for twenty years working at different hotels. He has come to Tetiaroa to serve the workers in the evenings and any guests who might visit the island. Marlon asks him questions, studies him. William comes by. He says he's been saving a very powerful palm wine drink for Marlon to taste. It's been fermenting six months. Brando says to bring it and we both have a glass. He tells me he's had some really wild parties on the island. "Once, we got six kinds of drunk, it went all night. Tahitians can drink, party, fuck, sleep, drink, party, fuck, all through the night. I can't do that. Once I'm drunk I'm out."

Apropos of nothing Marlon states, "Next to the gonads, the most important organs we have are our eyes. How ridiculous to put them right near where the fighting instrument is." He means the mouth. Where would he put the eyes? "The neck," he says. "But isn't that where an animal would go, for the neck?" I ask. "Well, you need three places," he mutters, but it occurs to him you need binary vision, thus two eyes must be in each place. It gets too complicated to figure out where one's eyes would be safest.

The one drink is enough for Marlon. He talks of psychics, mediums, and clairvoyants. They're mostly fakes, he says, but he believes in Peter Hurkos, who once came close to guessing what object Brando had carefully concealed inside a Lucite box which he had wrapped in twine. It was an old nail from the original "Bounty" that a bald-headed man had given to him. Hurkos said that the object was weathered and had been given to Brando by a balding man. "I could have put anything into that box," Marlon says, "a pig's knuckle, a fingernail." He's also interested in the parapsychological work of a former high school classmate of his, Dr. Thelma Moss of UCLA.

He asks William how to say red and yellow in Tahitian. Each word is pronounced twice. Marlon has always had a talent for languages.

After dinner we take a walk. There's a circle of light around the half moon. White birds dive into the water. The sky sparkles with stars and falling meteorites. I ask Marlon if a UFO landed in front of him would he go? Most celebrities I've asked that question—like Barbra Streisand or Dolly Parton—have said definitely not, they wouldn't take the risk of entering the unknown and *being* unknown. But Marlon says, "Of course." He doesn't believe that such things actually happen. "The odds that both we would be exploring space and space would be exploring us within a span of a thousand years would be incredible." That we've only been exploring for twenty-five years and there have been so many sightings makes him believe that our government is far more advanced than we know, and all those peculiar movements in the sky are secret experiments that the government has refused to reveal.

He picks up a handful of sand. "There are probably more individual grains in two handfuls of sand than there are stars in the universe," he says.

I've brought my tape recorder with me and turn it on. We talk for a while but I am distracted by what appears to be a white blur crossing over the lagoon. The second time it occurs I interrupt Marlon who jumps up like a shot anxious to see what I've seen. "Christ, why didn't you tell me? I can always talk." Once he and

Tarita were lying on the sand and she saw something blue rise out of the sea and come down again. She grabbed him tightly, digging her nails into his arm in fear. "I'm always looking for that sort of stuff," he says.

June 16: Day Four

We tape all afternoon, six hours. Brando's a bit pontifical at times but that's to be expected. Beginning sessions are usually strategy sessions. He must have caught two-dozen flies.

He gives me two things to read: the *Government Misconduct Associated with the Dennis Banks/Russell Means Wounded Knee Trial*, and the transcript of the trial proceedings of *United States v. Russell Means and Dennis Banks*.

At dinner he is quiet. He counts the newly inlaid wooden strips in the ceiling and wonders how long it will last. He breaks the silence with a question: "So what do you think's going to happen in Kananga?" Rhodesia might straighten itself out, he says, but South Africa is going to explode.

Afterwards, out on the pier, he watches the lagoon. "If you had a thirty-four-foot aluminum straw and you were going to suck up Fanta, you could only get it thirty-three feet because that's all a vacuum pump can pump," he says.

Then he gets on his belly and stares at the water. He's puzzled by changes in the current. He says he's never seen anything like it in the fifteen years he's been visiting his island. He seems very concerned.

June 17: Day Five

"Another day in paradise," Marlon says with a laugh at breakfast. He entertains Caroline's daughter by closing his eyes and swiping at a group of flies buzzing around the grapefruit. He asks her to guess how many he's caught. She says three. He flings them onto the floor and they count. Eight. While she is counting he catches another fly and pops it into his mouth. When she looks at him he opens his mouth and the fly comes out.

He spends the morning talking on his ham radio, using another name and never revealing his true identity. He talks with someone living underground conducting medical experiments at the South Pole. A man living five hundred miles west of Miami tells him how lightning once went through his phone and burned his wife's nose. A third connection is a man who is into contests. "I'm not really interested in talking about contests," Marlon says. One transmission clears up a mystery. Brando finds out that there was an earthquake in Samoa last night—the changing current he observed on the pier was the effect of a tidal wave caused by the quake.

He leaves the radio, listens for a moment, and says a plane is coming. I hear nothing for a minute, then the faint sound of an engine. Marlon tells me he has very sensitive hearing. He's been to doctors about it because even the hitting of a spoon on a cup can irritate him. The doctors told him there was nothing wrong. "You hear what you want to hear," they said. "Maybe that's so," Marlon says now, "maybe it is psychological. Because sometimes I can't hear what people are saying. I can hear high-pitched noises and sounds, but I can't hear human voices."

The plane lands, bringing his seventeen-year-old son Teihotu and some friends. Tomorrow is Father's Day and they have come from Papeete, where they are still in school, to spend a few days. Marlon and Tarita greet them, and then he returns to his bungalow as Tarita sweeps the compound. "I never saw anybody work as hard as Tarita," he says. "All she does is work."

We spend part of the day sitting on the sand looking out at the lagoon and the large coral rocks that form a line to break up any tall waves before they reach his bungalow. He spots a shell embedded in the rocks, gets a hammer and file, and starts banging out chunks of the coral to get at the shell. Then his daughter Cheyenne comes, bringing him some shells she has found. She is a beautiful, but moody, girl who speaks both English and French. Brando takes her shells and thanks her. When she runs off he says he saves everything she brings him.

I ask him if twenty years ago he could have lived the way he does now. He says no. "Once I was the only person here, absolutely alone on this island. I really like being alone," he says.

He goes inside, finds a strength-tester that measures the pressure it takes to make a light turn on, and says, "Here, you'll like this." He said Teihotu could do eighty-five pounds with both hands. I try. The light doesn't go on.

Towards evening I walk over to the bar and talk with George. I ask him if he knows who Marlon is. "An actor," George says. Is he aware that Brando's considered to be one of the world's greatest actors? "Auf, well, everybody's the greatest," George answers. "What I do, what he does, it's a business. He's an actor, I'm a bartender. People like me at what I do. I could be an actor."

June 18: Day Six

Although Marlon's feeling under the weather we are going on a picnic to another island. On the catamaran he asks, "How fast do you think we're going?" We all guess. "Twenty-two miles per hour," he answers, explaining that the catamaran goes twelve mph and the wind is adding another ten. He knows this because there are still flies on the boat and "flies can fly up to twenty-two miles per hour."

He gets out his Leicaflex and takes pictures of everyone. Focusing on Caroline, he says, "You've got snot in your nose." She almost falls for it.

A Tahitian who had trailed a line behind the catamaran hauls in a large fish. Then he removes the hook and chops the head. Brando is squeamish. "Isn't that horrible? But that's the nature of the beast. They don't want to eat cornflakes."

When we reach the other island Marlon asks Teihotu to carry him on his back, he doesn't want to get wet. Teihotu complies.

We gather wood and start a fire to keep the flies and mosquitoes away. Tarita and her crew go off to fish by the reef. Marlon watches them from his blanket. He picks up a crab, plays with it, wedging a sliver of wood between the crab and its shell so he can examine it.

"Do you think you could make the Brooklyn Bridge out of all the bottle caps in the world?" he asks. When I say yes, he says, "Boy, you're sure of that one, aren't you?"

Someone wants a Sprite, someone else a Fanta, but there is no bottle opener. Marlon uses a Coke bottle to open the Fanta by pushing one cap under the other. But the wrong bottle opens and the Coke explodes all over his face and clothing. "Anybody want Coke?" he deadpans.

Tarita and the others return with dozens of speargunned multicolored fish. After eating and drinking, they start packing things. Marlon sits. "Nobody ever says, 'Let's go,'" he says. "Everyone just knows when it's time to leave." Cheyenne brings him his Father's Day present: a drawing she's done of the sea.

At dinner, a Tahitian woman is softly crying, waiting for Marlon to finish eating. Marlon sees her and gets up. She has come to complain of her boyfriend "husband" who had beat her up. He had been drinking and when he entered the kitchen she told him to do the dishes. He refused and belted her. Marlon goes to tell the man if he does it again he must leave the island. "Why they come to me, I don't know," he says when he returns. "It's my bat and ball, I guess."

June 19: Day Seven

"I find him an extraordinary man," Caroline says at breakfast while Marlon sleeps late. "He has the most incredible memory for details which often seem unimportant to us—the way your nails were cut, how you sat, what you wore, the way your hand fell upon your cheek." She says that he remembers all of Cole Porter's and Harold Arlen's song lyrics. She says he's not hassled as much in Los Angeles as he is in New York, where people are always taking his picture. When he travels he always leaves behind his luggage, cameras, whizzing through the airport, leaving his secretary to handle customs. He hates waiting around.

Caroline, whose mother is Japanese and father English, has never seen *Streetcar* or *On the Waterfront*.

Marlon comes by in the afternoon, a glob of sun cream on his nose. It's hot, there's no wind, and he calls to William to knock out three more windows in my bungalow so the air can circulate better. He picks up my telescope, looks through it, and says, "This is a ten-power." I ask him how he knew and he talks about looking through it with one eye and opening the other eye and measuring the distance between both views. What he actually did was read on the telescope that it was ten-power.

As we walk back to his bungalow he says, "I bet Caroline you wouldn't say anything about this shit on my nose." "You won," I say.

He notices a large hole in a tree's branch. "That's where mosquitoes breed," he says, getting a shovel and filling the hole with sand, dirt, and a plant which he uproots.

That evening, another bet. Marlon says the dinner gong was beaten, Caroline says it wasn't. The loser has to stand on a table and sing and dance. They ask me if the signal had been given and I say yes. Marlon looks pleased and insists Caroline pay the bet. Embarrassed, she climbs onto a table and does a two-step while singing "Somewhere Over the Rainbow." After a few bars she gets down, but Marlon says, "No, you have to finish." She gets back onto the table. There is a cruel satisfaction in Marlon's eyes.

I ask him if he loses many bets. "No, I don't," he answers. "I've been very lucky."

When Caroline drinks a Coke, Marlon says she shouldn't because it's too fattening. "It is not," she says, "there are only eighty calories in a six-ounce glass." Marlon sees doubt in her eyes and jumps on her, claiming there are at least two hundred calories. He wants to bet. She's game. He comes up with this: the loser has to sell used tires on the corner of Mulholland and Laurel Canyon in L.A. during rush hour. When Caroline wants something more immediate he comes up with the loser having to interrupt William seven times in one day while he is talking with someone else, saying, "William, there's no toilet paper."

William is supervising the cutting of new windows. He has been on the island for six years and has seen many changes, "some good, some bad." Projects get started, abandoned, contractors come and go. Has he ever seen any of Marlon's films? "Yes, *The Godfather* I liked." Does Marlon remind him of the Godfather? "Oh yes, yes he does. Sometimes." Does he ever talk to Marlon about it? "No, he doesn't like to talk about movies. If you ever say anything he just changes the subject. But he's a good man to work for, I like him."

Eri, Marlon's cook, has also seen some of her boss's films. "Something in Mexico," she remembers. And "the movie with a trolley. A love story about a man and his wife and her sister. I liked that. He was very young then, slim." She's also seen an Elvis Presley movie once. "He was singing in Hawaii. He was very handsome." Can she distinguish between Marlon and Elvis as actors? "Oh, they're both very nice," she says.

June 20: Day Eight

Gauguin light. Toilet clogged, water off. Another slow day on Tetiaroa.

Ten Days on Brando's Island

From my window I see Caroline's daughter, both hands clutching a walkie-talkie with raised antenna making it almost as tall as she is. She is being led around the island by Marlon, who sits in his bungalow. "Where are you now?" I hear his voice ask. She shouts an answer. "Don't shout," he tells her, "it comes out garbled and I cannot tell you what to do." She whispers back, "I'm not yet at the turtle cage, Marlon."

In the evening Brando and I listen to classical music on cassettes and play chess. He's a bold player and wins every game. "Nobody knows what makes a good chess player," he says. "It doesn't have to do with intelligence, it has to do with a sense of space. Architects usually make good chess players." We screw around, placing pieces at random and playing; then he puts a cardboard shield between the halves of the board and we arrange our pieces any way we want. Removes the cardboard, makes his first move, captures my queen. "Fate's fickle finger has come knocking on your door," he says.

He tells a story about Humphrey Bogart, who played a sadistic game of chess. ("Sadistic," along with "boring," are two of Brando's favorite words.) Once Bogie was set up by some friends who watched him always beat one of the guys on the set. They "wired" the guy and brought in a chess master, who hid in a room above them with a pair of binoculars, telling the guy how to move. As Bogie was losing he got so angry he upset the table and stormed out.

"Being proud is a sickness," Marlon says. "You have to always win, you can never lose. I was like that for a long time. People who always have to win usually have a lot of anxiety, they're very anxious people."

June 21: Day Nine

On an island like this, with little to do, one concentrates on minutiae. A fly walks over my hand; I study its wing structure, its eyes, head, body, and the cilia hair on its legs. A mosquito flies by, I notice its black and white stripes. Watch the way a worker uses a broom, the shuffle of his walk. Notice nature: how the sea moves, the wind bends the palms. For a man obsessed with details, as Brando is, an island heightens that obsession.

We tape until dinner, go night sailing afterwards. The moon is full, Caroline and her daughter join us. We wear bathing suits. Marlon wears a yellow waterproof windbreaker with hood, rubber pants, and boots. Looks like he came out of a chewing tobacco ad. We pull out the Hobie Cat and distribute our weight as Marlon does the sailing. We move fast in the wind. After an hour something on the mast snaps and steering becomes difficult. We pull in.

Back at his bungalow, during our last taped session, Marlon avoids questions about how much pain is involved in being an actor. He'd rather talk about women with big asses, which he prefers to women with small ones. "A woman with a small ass I treat almost as if she's paralytic." He tells me stories about women in his past. One woman plastered his poster from *Streetcar* all over her walls. She'd call him all the time when he lived in an apartment in Greenwich Village. She wouldn't tell him her name for six months, but said that she made her money by robbing people. She told him she and a friend were into cannibalism and they could take him to a place in New Jersey where they would eat him. That was sufficiently bizarre for him to at least find out who she was, so he told her to come by his place. When she did, he opened the door slightly with the chain in place, and told her to put both her hands through the door, where he grabbed them and then frisked her for a gun. When he let her in she took out a wad of bills and asked if he needed money. She was into a heavy Jesus trip and Marlon was her Christ. She was Mary Magdalene. She wanted to wash his feet. "Yeah," Marlon agreed, "I guess I can get into that fantasy." So she did, which aroused him. "I started feeling her body, undressing her, playing with her tits. She got all trembly, started shaking. I got excited and tried to fuck her. I don't remember if I did or not, if I got it in or not, because she was just shaking like a leaf."

Then she got *real* weird. She'd call him, stand outside his door, wouldn't leave him alone. This went on for years. He talked about her to his shrink and got her to go see him too. The shrink said the girl had a "fixation complex" and if rejected she could get violent. She was psychotic and dangerous. Marlon had a friend of his begin trailing her. Once she called him from a phone booth, and he told her he didn't want to see her anymore. The girl, according to his friend's report, started to pound the phone booth, breaking the glass, cutting herself up. Then she went to her apartment, took down all her *Streetcar Named Desire* posters, and burned them outside. She stood and stared at the rubble for a few hours.

Sometimes Marlon gets a vague, distant look in his eyes and stares out at the sea. Questions go unanswered. He says he doesn't have any ambition left, doesn't want to do the major plays, act for the sake of acting. He doesn't feel he has to prove himself. As Orson Welles once said, you don't have to repeat yourself to show you can still do it. The fact that you've done it is enough.

June 22: Day Ten

The plane comes in the morning. Marlon is still asleep. We had talked until 2 A.M. When I said goodnight he walked me to the door, polite, tired, a gracious host.

I fly to Tahiti with Tarita. She gives me a ride to my hotel. I ask her which she prefers, living on the island or in the city. "Here," she says, "in the city. He would like me to stay there. Once I stayed there two months. When he's not there it gets lonely. That's no kind of life."

Tarita acted in *Mutiny on the Bounty* and is still an attractive woman with a strong face. I ask if she'd like to be in more movies. "No," she says. Then, "Well, I would like, but he doesn't want me to. He wants me to stay home and raise the children."

At the hotel I kiss both her cheeks and say goodbye. Wondering if the mermaids will ever sing for Marlon Brando.

OTHER BOOKS BY LAWRENCE GROBEL

THE HUSTONS

When John Huston died at 81 on August 28, 1987, America lost a towering figure in movie history. The director of such classic films as *The Treasure of the Sierra Madre, The African Queen, The Maltese Falcon, Prizzi's Honor*, and *The Dead*, John Huston evoked passionate responses from everyone he encountered. He was at the center of a dynasty, with three generations of Oscar winners (Walter, John and Anjelica). Now the complete story of this remarkable family is told in *The Hustons*. The book chronicles the family's history—from Walter's days on the vaudeville circuit and his later fame on Broadway, through John's meteoric rise, to Anjelica's and Danny's emergence as formidable actors in film today. Grobel interviewed John Huston for over 100 hours and conducted 200 interviews with John's four children, three of his five wives, many of his mistresses, producers, writers, technicians, and a number of celebrities who rarely grant interviews. Larry King thought it, "Biography writing at its absolute best." Frederick Raphael wrote, "*The Hustons* is a delicious, wicked guide to the delicious, wicked life of a sly, sadistic scoundrel who was equaled only by Byron in the sentimental cynicism and fecund carelessness with which he played the world's game." Alyn Brodsky in *The Miami Herald* called it, "An engrossing study in family dynamics... Marvelous...This is one of the best biographies of a Hollywood personality since—actually, I can't recall since when." And the *Hollywood Reporter* said it "Reads like a gutsy movie that might have been made by Huston himself."

CONVERSATIONS WITH CAPOTE

Six months after Truman Capote died in 1984, *Conversations with Capote* was published and reached the top of best-seller lists in both New York and San Francisco. *The Philadelphia Inquirer* called it "A gossip's delight...full of scandalous comments about the rich and the famous." *Parade* called it "An engrossing read. Bitchy, high-camp opinions... from a tiny terror who wore brass knuckles on his tongue." *People* found it "Juicy stuff... provocative and entertaining...vintage Capote." Said the *San Francisco Chronicle*, "All the rumors you ever heard about Capote are here... Refreshing ...thoughtful and reflective." Grobel talked to Capote over a period of two years and it remains an essential part of the Capote canon.

CONVERSATIONS WITH BRANDO

Playboy named Lawrence Grobel "The Interviewer's Interviewer" for his uncanny ability to get America's greatest and most reclusive actor, Marlon Brando, to speak openly for the first time. When Grobel expanded the interview into a book, *American Cinematographer* said it "penetrates the complex nature of a very private man, probing his feelings on women and sex, Native Americans, corporate America and the FBI." James A. Michener thought it "explained Brando accurately: the torment, the arrogance—almost willed towards self-destruction—but above all, the soaring talent." And Elmore Leonard wrote, "Brando tells Larry Grobel what he won't discuss, but before you know it, they're talking about the forbidden subjects in depth. Amazing. How does Grobel do it?"

CONVERSATIONS WITH MICHENER

After successfully publishing his book-length interviews with Truman Capote and Marlon Brando, Grobel approached author James A. Michener as his next subject, and wound up taping their discussions over a 17 year period, right up until the last week of Michener's life. The result is the most comprehensive of all Grobel's "Conversation" books. Michener, who didn't start writing novels until he was 40, was a true citizen of the world. He foresaw the future of countries as diverse as Afghanistan, Poland, Japan, Spain, Hungary, Mexico, Israel, and the U.S. His books—like *Hawaii, The Source, Iberia, Sayonara*, and *Tales of the South Pacific*—sold millions of copies and many were made into films or TV miniseries. *Conversations with*

Other Books

Michener is as relevant today as it was prescient when it first appeared in 1999.

AL PACINO in Conversation with Lawrence Grobel

For more than a quarter century, Al Pacino has spoken freely and deeply with Lawrence Grobel on subjects as diverse as childhood, acting, and fatherhood. Here are the complete conversations and shared observations between the actor and the writer; the result is an intimate and revealing look at one of the most accomplished, and private, artists in the world, as Grobel and Pacino leave few stones unturned. *Al Pacino* is an intensely personal window into the life of an artist concerned more with the process of his art than with the fruits of his labor—a creative genius at the peak of his artistic powers who, after all these years, still longs to grow and learn more about his craft.

"I WANT YOU IN MY MOVIE!"
My Acting Debut & Other Misadventures Filming Al Pacino's *Wilde Salome*

"Why *am* I doing this?" Al Pacino wondered a year into his personal movie about his obsession with *Salome,* Oscar Wilde's lyrical play, written in 1891. "No one saw *Looking for Richard*, who's going to want to see something about Oscar Wilde?"

In *"I Want You in My Movie!"* Grobel found the answer to that question and more when he joined the crew and followed the creative process of filmmaking from inception to completion. His meticulous journal is as close to being there as a reader can ever hope to get. This intimate peek behind the curtain, documenting the hopes, dreams, frustrations and complexities of Pacino and all the people who come in and out of his life, is a fitting sequel to Grobel's internationally acclaimed *AL PACINO in Conversation with Lawrence Grobel*, which was named the Best International Book of the Year by the Society of French Film Critics. *"I Want You in My Movie!"* takes you deeper into the mind and process of Al Pacino. It's a movie buff's delight, warts and all.

THE ART OF THE INTERVIEW: Lessons from a Master of the Craft

J.P. Donleavy called Grobel, "the most intelligent interviewer in the United States." In *The Art of the Interview*, Grobel reveals the most memorable stories from his career, along with examples of the most candid moments from his long list of famous interviewees, from Oscar-winning actors and Nobel laureates to Pulitzer Prize-winning writers and sports figures. Taking us step-by-step through the interview process, from research and question writing to final editing, *The Art of the Interview* is a treat for journalists and culture vultures alike.

SIGNING IN: 50 Celebrity Profiles

From 2005—2010 Lawrence Grobel wrote over 50 magazine articles about his in-depth encounters with some of the most famous people in the world. Each piece had only one caveat: to include at least a paragraph about something the celebrity had signed. So Grobel built each portrait around a signed photo, poster, drawing, personal letter, or book inscription, many of which are shown in this engaging book. Among the entertainers and writers included are Barbra Streisand, Marlon Brando, Al Pacino, Farrah Fawcett, Henry Fonda, Madonna, Angelina Jolie, Robin Williams, Steve Martin, Luciano Pavarotti, Anthony Kiedis, Truman Capote, Monica Lewinsky, Norman Mailer, Elmore Leonard, and Saul Bellow.

ICONS

When the editors of *Trendy* magazine in Poland asked celebrated journalist Lawrence Grobel to write detailed cover stories about some of the Hollywood icons he's known and written about over the years, Grobel took the opportunity to profile fifteen internationally beloved stars: Jack Nicholson, Angelina Jolie, Halle Berry, Anthony Hopkins, Kim Basinger, Anthony Kiedis, Jodie Foster, Nicole Kidman, Cameron Diaz, Meryl Streep, Gwyneth Paltrow, Tom Waits, Penelope Cruz, Sharon Stone, and Robert De Niro. Each profile is illustrated with the hip *Trendy* cover.

YOU SHOW ME YOURS: A Memoir

Lawrence Grobel's energetic memoir, takes the reader on a wild, improbable, and highly charged ride.

It begins with him growing up on the streets of Brooklyn, where he was nearly kidnapped as an infant, and the suburbs of Long Island, where his sex education began at a very early age. By the age of 15, he was competing with his best friend over a modern day Lolita. A serious prankster long before the *Jackass* movies, Grobel was scaring the daylights out of gullible friends and disbelieving adults. But he also marched with Dr. King in Mississippi under a hail of bullets, and came of age under the guidance of an enlightened Mexican Don Juan. After graduating from UCLA, he joined the Peace Corps, which afforded him the chance to communicate with a fetish high priestess in Ghana, pygmies in Uganda, and stoned-out hippies on the island of Lamu. In the '70s he became a New Journalist, covering stories like the Demolition Derbies, Transcendental Meditation, Sky Diving, Sailplane Gliding, Archery and Karate. When he left New York for California he turned his skills to celebrity interviews. Starting with Mae West, Linus Pauling, Ray Bradbury and Jane Fonda for *Newsday*, he moved on to conducting over 50 interviews for *Playboy*.

It's a journey through the Looking Glass of American Culture from the post-War '50s, the sexually liberated '60s, the Civil Rights movement, and the "Me Decade." Diane Keaton calls this book "Profoundly entertaining and totally INSANE!" It is all of that, and then some. We leave him on a weeklong interview assignment in Tetioroa, Tahiti with Marlon Brando, with a promise of things to come.

Other Books

MADONNA PAINTS A MUSTACHE & Other Celebrity Observations (Poetry)

"Elliott Gould said to Elvis Presley/'I may be crazy, but/What's that gun doing/ Sitting on your hip?'"

"Mae West always made an entrance/Even when exiting."

For 40 years Lawrence Grobel has interviewed some of the world's most talented and famous people and after each encounter he wrote a short poem crystallizing his insights and impressions. Tart, funny, sensitive, always succinct and sometimes downright scandalous, he filed them away. Until now. In this anthology of more than 150 poems, this jaunty dish on the rich and famous targets all these topics with attitude: Relationships, Mysticism, Paranoia, Bad Behavior, Race, Sex, Religion, and Gambling. These titles give a clue as to content: Madonna Paints a Mustache; James Franco was Pretty Crank-O; Dolly Parton at 3 A.M.; Drew Barrymore Keeps Her First Gray Hair; Saul Bellow Quite a Fellow; I'd Like to Say I Had a Ball Jake Gyllenhaal; Penelope Cruz Nothing to Lose; Ashley Judd Spits Tobacco; Nicole Kidman Brought Sushi; Bud Cort's His Harold Past; Zsa Zsa Ain't So Ga-Ga; Bruce Springsteen Gets Rejected; When Christian Slater Got Out of Jail; 14 Carat Goldie; I Kissed Farrah Fawcett; I'd Rather Be Alone, Sharon Stone.

ABOVE THE LINE: Conversations About the Movies

Above the Line is a dazzling gathering of insights and anecdotes from all corners of the film industry—interviews that reveal the skills, intelligence, experiences, and emotions of eleven key players who produce, write, direct, act in, and review the movies: Oliver Stone, Anthony Hopkins, Jodie Foster, Robert Evans, Lily Tomlin, Jean-Claude Van Damme, Harrison Ford, Robert Towne, Sharon Stone, and Siskel and Ebert. Witty, scathing, gossipy, generous, the interviewees show just what make the movies work from "above the line"—from the perspective of those whose names go above the title. Each of these gifted individuals represents a piece of the puzzle that gives rise to some of the best in moviemaking today.

ENDANGERED SPECIES: Writers Talk about Their Craft, Their Visions, Their Lives

Norman Mailer once told Lawrence Grobel that writers may be an endangered species. And Saul Bellow told him, "The country has changed so, that what I do no longer signifies anything, as it did when I was young." But to judge from this collection, writers and writing aren't done for quite yet. Sometimes serious, sometimes funny, sometimes caustic, always passionate, the twelve writers in *Endangered Species* (Bellow, Mailer, Ray Bradbury, J.P. Donleavy, James Ellroy, Allen Ginsberg, Andrew Greeley, Alex Haley, Joseph

Heller, Elmore Leonard, Joyce Carol Oates, and Neil Simon) memorably state their case for what they do and how they do it. And they even offer an opinion or two about other writers and about the entire publishing food chain: from agents to publishers to booksellers to critics to readers.

CONVERSATIONS WITH ROBERT EVANS

"I don't want to have a slow death," Robert Evans told Lawrence Grobel. "That's my fear. I've had a gun put in my mouth, a gun put at my temple. I've had a gun put on me five different times to talk, and not once have I ever talked." But talk is what Evans does in his conversations with Grobel which director Brett Ratner published in 2009. As the head of Paramount Studios in the 1970s Evans produced some of the most iconic movies of that era, including *Love Story, The Odd Couple, Paper Moon, True Grit, Catch 22, Chinatown,* and *The Godfather*. But his life was much more than that of a movie producer and this book is eye-opening in its honesty and its finger-pointing.

CLIMBING HIGHER

A New York Times Bestseller, *Climbing Higher* is the story of Montel Williams' life and personal struggles with MS. In 1999, after almost 20 years of mysterious symptoms that he tried to ignore, Montel Williams, a decorated former naval intelligence officer and Emmy Award-winning talk show host, was finally diagnosed with multiple sclerosis. Like others suffering from the devastating and often disabling disease, which attacks the central nervous system, Montel was struck with denial, fear, depression, and anger. Yet somehow he emerged with a fierce determination not to be beaten down by MS, and to live the most vital and productive life possible while becoming a dedicated spokesperson and fundraiser for the disease. *Climbing Higher* is a penetrating and insightful look at a remarkable man, his extraordinary career, and the tumultuous life that graced him with hard-won courage and wisdom. In addition, with the help of a team of leading doctors, *Climbing Higher* offers up-to-the-minute information on new MS research and invaluable guidance for managing MS.

MARILYN & ME

In 1960 and 1962 Lawrence Schiller was asked by *Paris Match* and *Life* magazines to photograph Marilyn Monroe on the set of *Let's Make Love* and *Something's Got to Give*, which was never completed because of her controversial death. Schiller had befriended Monroe and he asked Lawrence Grobel to help him shape the story of that friendship into this memoir. It's a new addition to the Monroe saga from the perspective of an impressionistic young photographer and the iconic sex symbol.

Yoga? No! SHMOGA!

Google "Yoga" and 103,000,000 items come up. One hundred and three *million*! Yet for everyone who practices yoga, there are dozens of others who just sit and watch. *Yoga? No! Shmoga!* is for those who sit and watch, as well as for those who actually do yoga and have a sense of humor. Best-selling author Lawrence Grobel has ventured into satire with this look at the lighter side of yoga. Shmoga is the Lazy Man's Way to Inner Peace. It's like a non-diet book for ice cream lovers. In 43 short chapters it pokes fun at sports, religion, exercise, Wall Street, art, entertainment, and people looking for an excuse to not do anything more than lift a finger. Yoga wives can give it to their couch-potato husbands. Or those husbands can give it to their wives to show them why fiddling with the remote is safer (and thus healthier!) than strenuous stretching into unnatural shapes. Often absurd, sometimes profound, and always whimsical, in this world full of books that focus on discipline and self-improvement, this is a breath of fresh air. Though a satire, there is a lot of wisdom in *Yoga? No! Shmoga!* And some very good advice. It teaches you to take charge of your life, but in a very clever way. Doing Shmoga actually makes sense!

CATCH A FALLEN STAR (a novel)

Catch a Fallen Star is the story of Layton Cross, a man who fails upward. It's a private look at the fast-paced life of an actor who achieved stardom after marrying a superstar, only to unravel as she outshone him. His career sinks from bad films to worse TV and an embarrassing stint in the theater–yet his fame and popularity continue to rise. As his battles with his two ex-wives go public, he becomes embroiled in family problems, deceitful friends, devious journalists, and cunning studio heads. Grobel, whose in-depth interviews have appeared in *Playboy, Movieline, Premiere*, and *Rolling Stone*, is on familiar territory with this novel.

BEGIN AGAIN FINNEGAN (a novel)
How far would you go to help your best friend?

That's the question journalist Devin Hunter faces when movie star Adrian Kiel asks him to be his alibi to cover a possible murder. Devin's decision starts a chain of events that spiral out of control as he tries to hold the pieces of his life together.

This is a story about secret lives, psychiatric wards, celebrity "justice," buccal onanism, blackmail, betrayal and a modern day take on James Joyce in exile; but mostly it's about relationships and their consequences. It explores the loyalty of a friendship that increasingly appears one-sided and slowly implodes. The action is fast paced, with twists to the plot at every corner. The cast of characters runs the gamut of fawning fans to million-dollar lawyers and crooked accountants. It's set in Hollywood, and peels back the glamour of that town to reveal the snake pit underneath.

THE BLACK EYES OF AKBAH (a novella)
After leaving Ghana, where they served for two years in the Peace Corps, Eric and Anika agree to travel together to Kenya and India to get to know each other better and

see if they want to spend the rest of their lives together. They agree to work their way across the Indian Ocean on a cargo ship ominously called The Black Eyes of Akbah. The crew is a melting pot of all the indigenous peoples of the region. They leave Mombasa for Mumbai, but the chilling terror that happens along the way will change the way they see each other and the world they thought they knew. Oliver Stone compared this story to a cross between *The African Queen* and *Midnight Express*.

COMMANDO EX (a novella)

Commando Ex is a wild Australian hedonist racing across Africa on his Motoguzzi motorcycle, chasing thrills and adventure, living life to the max and flaunting what you can be if you're absolutely free. "He's the cream of the freedom crop….nerve tingling the moments and bojangling experiences." This is nothing like any of Grobel's other books. It's wordplay on steroids. It's exotic, erotic, and funny, as it follows "the lives and times, the lays and plays, the huck and suck of an antsy chancy ice cream cone of a fella….a galactic whirlwind of a self-proclaimed Commando" who has "not a peep or a beep of quiet in his veins." He's someone who "flies around like Dali dangling from the ends of his mustache, not bothering with the rites of culture or the sounds of one hand clapping." His gospel is "Only one life, one life, one life. A cry and a scream if it's lived at a loss, if it's misused and tossed, too planned, double-crossed" and believes that "with a little muscle and a lot of hustle you could become king of the hog pile, steal all the time it takes to live a full life and go out and buzz burn bull and bellow—the philosophy of the fellow." After all, "What's to lose? An army to grab you? A desk job to nail you? A mechanic to jail you? Chuck it. Change your name, change the game, steal on a boat and float all the way to foreign places." Which is what this singular comic book of a character does. It's a wild, uniquely styled story of a never lonely, one-and-only, who bites and grabs everything that comes his way. "So keep up, speed along, trip flip and skip through the one life worth living, the fully explored, high geared unfeared not scared life of the Commando. Sight...on!"

Printed in Great Britain
by Amazon.co.uk, Ltd.,
Marston Gate.